BestMasters

Springer awards "BestMasters" to the best application-oriented master's theses, which were completed at renowned chairs of economic sciences in Germany, Austria, and Switzerland in 2013.

The works received highest marks and were recommended for publication by supervisors. As a rule, they show a high degree of application orientation and deal with current issues from different fields of economics.

The series addresses practitioners as well as scientists and offers guidance for early stage researchers.

Carolin Proft

The Speed of Human and Task Integration in Mergers and Acquisitions

Human Integration as Basis for Task Integration

Springer Gabler

Carolin Proft
Innsbruck, Austria

Masterthesis Management Center Innsbruck, Austria, 2013

ISBN 978-3-658-04563-0 ISBN 978-3-658-04564-7 (eBook)
DOI 10.1007/978-3-658-04564-7

The Deutsche Nationalbibliothek lists this publication in the Deutsche Nationalbibliografie; detailed bibliographic data are available in the Internet at http://dnb.d-nb.de.

Library of Congress Control Number: 2013955731

Springer Gabler

Printed on acid-free paper

Springer Gabler is a brand of Springer DE.
Springer DE is part of Springer Science+Business Media.
www.springer-gabler.de

Geleitwort

Mergers & Acquisitions (M&A) sind ein zentrales Element des strategischen Managements und der Unternehmensentwicklung. Durch akquisitorisches Wachstum können Unternehmen schneller auf marktseitige Entwicklungen reagieren, als dies mit organischem Wachstum möglich wäre. Nichts desto trotz vernichten ein Großteil der Transaktionen eher Wert, als dass sie tatsächlich Wert schaffen. Bislang gelang es der akademischen Forschung nicht, umfassend die Ursachen der Wertvernichtung zu erklären. Dennoch besteht in der Literatur große Einigkeit darüber, dass die Integrationsphase entscheidend für das Gelingen einer Transaktion ist. Erst durch die Integration kann eine Interaktion der beteiligten Unternehmen erfolgen und die prognostizierten Synergien gehoben sowie redundante Ressourcen eliminiert werden.

Das Thema der Integrationsgeschwindigkeit erfährt von Seiten der Praxis große Aufmerksamkeit, dennoch wird es von der akademischen Forschung weitestgehend ignoriert. An dieser Stelle setzt die Arbeit von Carolin Proft an. Nach einer umfassenden theoretischen Aufarbeitung des Themas, lassen sich klare Forschungsfelder identifizieren. Die Darstellung der Integration als eine Abfolge sequenzieller Prozesse auf unterschiedlichen organisationalen Ebenen mit unterschiedlichen Integrationsgeschwindigkeiten ermöglicht deutlich detaillierte Einblicke als die bestehende Diskussion um schnelle oder langsame Integration.

Die Trennung von Human und Task Integrationsgeschwindigkeit ist ein entscheidender Mehrwert der Arbeit von Frau Proft. Auf Basis des Literaturreview lassen sich klare Forschungshypothesen ableiten. Diese Hypothesen werden durch eine quantitative empirische Primärdatenuntersuchung getestet. Das Vorgehen bei der empirischen Untersuchung entspricht den internationalen akademischen Standards. In Summe konnte Frau Proft 101 Führungskräfte von Käuferunternehmen aus der DACH Region befragen. Bevor die Hypothesen verifiziert bzw. falsifiziert werden, testet die Autorin mögliche Verzerrungen der Datengrundlage. Neben Non-or Late Response Bias wird auch ein möglicher Common Method Bias getestet. Ein potentieller Key Informant Bias kann nicht zur Gänze ausgeschlossen werden.

Die entwickelten Hypothesen werden mithilfe von OLS Regressionen getestet. Frau Proft kann in Ihrer Arbeit nachweisen, dass Human und Task Integrationsgeschwindigkeiten unterschiedliche Wirkungen haben und dass die zeitliche Abfolge beider Integrationsebenen erfolgsentscheidend ist. Daher gelingt es der Autorin, neue Erkenntnisse zu erzielen, die dazu in der Lage sind, die sehr heterogenen Erkenntnisse der Forschung zu erklären.

Neben der Relevanz für zukünftige Forschungsarbeiten sind die Ergebnisse der Arbeit auch für die Praxis von großer Bedeutung. Daher bleibt der Arbeit von Frau Proft zu wünschen, dass sie die breite und interessierte Leserschaft findet, die ihr zweifelsohne zusteht.

Dr. Florian Bauer

MCI Management Center Innsbruck

Das Management Center Innsbruck (MCI) ist integraler Bestandteil des in Österreich einzigartigen Konzepts "Offene Universität Innsbruck". Die Idee zur Gründung des MCI wurde Anfang der 1990er Jahre von der Universität Innsbruck im Zuge der baulichen Errichtung und inhaltlichen Weiterentwicklung der Sozial- und Wirtschaftswissenschaftlichen Fakultät geboren.

Das MCI begleitet motivierte Menschen, die ihre Zukunft durch zielgerichtete akademische Aus- und Weiterbildung aktiv gestalten wollen, in ihrer beruflichen und persönlichen Entwicklung.

Führungskräften und Nachwuchsführungskräften der unterschiedlichen Managementebenen und Branchen bietet das MCI Bachelor-Studiengänge, Master-Studiengänge sowie Executive Master-Studiengänge, Zertifikatslehrgänge, Seminare, wissenschaftliche Foren und maßgeschneiderte Firmentrainings.

Die am MCI vermittelten Inhalte umfassen wirtschaftlich und gesellschaftlich relevantes Wissen auf wissenschaftlichem Niveau und mit hoher Praxisrelevanz. Als international ausgerichtete Hochschule geht das MCI offen auf neue Perspektiven, Methoden und Aufgabenstellungen zu. Konstruktiver Dialog und das gemeinschaftliche Erarbeiten interdisziplinärer Handlungskompetenz zählen zu den tragenden Säulen des Lehrens und Lernens am MCI.

Als Unternehmerische Hochschule® fördert das MCI die Wettbewerbsfähigkeit von Organisationen und leistet einen Beitrag zur Professionalisierung von Wirtschaft, Verwaltung, Politik und Kultur. Angewandte Forschung & Entwicklung und die Förderung von Technologie, Innovation und Unternehmensgründung nehmen am MCI zunehmende Bedeutung ein, stärken den Wirtschaftsstandort und tragen zur Sicherung einer qualitätsorientierten Lehre bei.

Eingebettet in ein breites Netzwerk von Trägern, Förderern und Partnern ist das MCI wichtiger Motor in der Positionierung Innsbrucks, Tirols und Österreichs als Zentrum für wissenschaftliche Auseinandersetzung und internationale Begegnung.

Der synergetische Verbund mit der Universität Innsbruck, die Nähe zur lebendigen Innsbrucker Altstadt und die kraftvolle Architektur des Standorts sind Ausdruck für die Philosophie und den Auftrag dieses international wirkenden Hochschulzentrums.

Acknowledgement

I would like to express my deepest appreciation to all of the individuals who provided me with their assistance developing the master thesis and its completion.

My special gratitude refers to Dr. Florian A. Bauer who contributed the greatest share to my master thesis. Without his continuous suggestions, patience and support, this thesis would not have been possible. Thanks to his willingness to share his knowledge, I have gained enormous insights into quantitative analysis and the thrilling world of mergers and acquisitions. In addition, his passion with regard to scientific work strengthened my interest in the field of scientific research.

I would like to thank my research group. Their help and sense of purpose paved the way to a successful data collection and analysis respectively. It was a pleasure to share ideas, insights and knowledge. Additionally, I want to thank the experts within our pretest group who contributed to the quality of our questionnaire and overall study. This also refers to all of the companies who invested their time and effort in order to provide sufficient data.

It is a great pleasure to thank Sheila Murphy and Klaus Schmerler who proofread my work and shared their critical thoughts with respect to my paper. Finally, I am truly grateful to have such a great family, a patient boyfriend and amazing friends supporting me in course of my studies.

Carolin Proft

List of Content

List of Tables

List of Figures

List of Abbreviations

CEE	Central and Eastern Europe
CEO	Chief Executive Officer
CFO	Chief Financial Officer
DACH	Germany, Austria, Switzerland
DM	Deutsche Mark
EUR	Euro
HR	Human Resources
IPO	Initial Public Offering
IT	Information Technology
M&A	Mergers and Acquisitions
R&D	Research and Development
ROA	Return on Assets
ROE	Return on Equity
ROI	Return on Investment
UK	United Kingdom
USA	United States of America
USD	United States Dollar

1 Introduction

As an introduction to the topic of mergers and acquisitions (M&A), chapter 1 outlines the significance of the topic. This chapter presents the initial situation, followed by the illustration of the research objectives and continues to outline the structure of the paper.

1.1 Initial Situation

Driven by the motivating equation one plus one equals three (Marks & Mirvis, 2010, p. 2), various managers opt for the corporate combination of mergers or acquisitions. As compared to other strategic combinations like alliances and franchising, mergers and acquisitions provide the highest level of control, impact and integration (Marks & Mirvis, 2010, p. 12). M&A strategy paves the way to protect company's own market share and competitive advantage when facing the steadily increasing pressure of globalization (Marks & Mirvis, 2001, p. 80). Management is well aware of those benefits. Despite many uncertainties in the current economic market and the drop in M&A turnover volume in 2008 (Behringer, 2013, p. 29), M&A activity is expected to increase in the year of 2013. According to a study across US companies conducted by Isom and colleagues, environmental conditions such as company liquidity, low interest rates and the availability of debt in beneficial terms (Isom, Madden, Moyers, & Tiemann, 2013, p. 2) promote the M&A activities. Based on those external conditions, 35% of the respondents say that they are more optimistic with respect to the deal environment in 2013 compared to 2012 (Isom et al., 2013, p.2). The present M&A market shows furthermore a change in the acquisition behavior of managers. In fact, buyer companies choose their target companies more carefully and show more awareness with respect to their liability of M&A activities as compared to 2008 (Kary, 2013, p. 11). However, in analyzing the concept of M&A activities, it is essential to take into consideration the two sides of the coin. Failure rates range from 40-60% (Appelbaum, Gandell, Yortis, Proper, & Jobin, 2000, p. 649; Datta, 1991, p. 281), some studies even argue for a failure rate of 80-90% (Christensen, Alton, Rising, & Waldeck, 2011, p. 49). Various studies have been engaging into in-depth analysis of factors that influence the M&A activity and performance. However, failure rate did not change until today

(Behringer, 2013, p. 29). The facts and figures of the present M&A activity show an urgent call for action. It is arguable that M&A literature failed to uncover decisive factors that influence and promote the M&A performance.

1.2 Aim of the Research

An important stream of thinking within the vast M&A research reflects on the post-merger integration process. From a practical perspective, speed of integration should be seen as an essential tool to influence the M&A performance in a positive way. In a study conducted by Mergermarket (2007), managers were asked about what they would have done differently with regard to their integration management. Retrospectively, 25% of the respondents said they would have integrated much quicker than actually realized (Mergermarket, 2007, p. 12). In a paradoxical manner, the vast body of M&A literature largely neglected this field of research (Homburg & Bucerius, 2006, p. 347). The main arguments presented in this body of literature rely on the idea that all value creation takes place within the integration process (Haspeslagh & Jemison, 1991, p. 121). Generally, research approaches such topics in three steps: analyze management integration actions, understand the effect on buyer and target company, and describe under which circumstances this process leads to value creation (Homburg & Bucerius, 2006, p. 347). This paper particularly builds on previous studies that analyzed the post integration process with respect to speed (Bauer, 2013, pp. 1-9; Birkinshaw, Bresman, & Hakanson, 2000, pp. 365-425). My study aims answering the question "what pace of integration is needed in order to increase the M&A success rate?". I believe that the study is unique in two ways: It first analyzes quantitatively the effect of speed of integration on M&A performance by separating the integration process into two subgroups: task integration speed and human integration speed. To be more precise, I replaced the question "Is speed of integration beneficial to M&A success" with "Which type of speed of integration is beneficial for M&A success?". It therefore combines the process school and organizational school of thought (Birkinshaw et al., 2000, p. 399). This split of task and human integration speed is especially of importance because the whole integration phase is regarded a "multi-faceted process" (Epstein, 2004, p. 175). To my knowledge, only one single study conducted by Bauer (2013) conducted this type of study wherein the moderating effect of acquisition experience for task and human integration speed and its influence on M&A performance was identified (Bauer, Degischer, & Matzler, 2013, pp. 1-9). Secondly, the model assessment is unique as it uses the established measurement model for relative speed conducted by Bauer (2012) and proves its efficiency (Bauer & Matzler, 2012, p. 17). The study aims at providing a deeper insight into the complex field of speed of integration, its interrelation on a company's organizational levels and consequently its influence on the overall M&A performance.

1.3 Structure

In order to reach the intended goal and provide for a solid and profound literature contribution, the paper is structured in five main parts (see Table 1):

Structure		
1. Introduction		
1.1 Initial situation	1.2 Aim of research	1.3 Structure
2. State of the art		
2.1 Merger and acquisitions	2.2 M&A post-merger integration	2.3 Problem statement
3. Research model and hypotheses development		
3.1 Research model	3.2 Hypotheses development	
4. Methodology		
4.1 Measurement development	4.2 Sample and data	4.3 Results
5. Discussion		
5.1 Managerial implications	5.2 Theoretical implications	5.3 Limitations and future research

Table 1 Structure of the Paper
Own elaboration

The first section introduces the general topic of M&A by referring to its initial situation, the objectives of the paper and by briefly summarizing the structure. Section two provides a solid basis of the topic of merger and acquisitions and outlines aspects with respect to the importance, types of strategic combinations, categorizations of M&A's, four schools of thought, M&A processes and motives and objectives of M&A's. The topic becomes more narrow with section 2.2 where I will introduce post-merger integration, the decisive integration phase with respect to value creation. This topic will analyze the degree of integration, human integration, task integration and finally the central topic of the paper speed of integration. Section 2.3 states the actual problem while providing a short literature overview, discussing challenges with respect to speed of integration and finally presenting the research gap. In order to fill the gap, the subsequent section encompasses all issues related to methodology: First of all I will demonstrate the measurement development by presenting the independent variables, dependent variables and control variables. As a next step, I will roughly present the sample as well as the data used for the study. Based on those figures, section 4.3 provides descriptive statistics including sample description, and the testing on validity and reliability. I will then evaluate the research model and test the hypotheses established in section 3. After summarizing the results of section 4, the last chapter discusses the findings. First managerial implications are analyzed followed by theoretical implications. The paper closes with future research recommendation.

2 State of the Art

Chapter two aims at providing a theoretical framework that forms the basis for all of the following chapters. Therefore basic concepts of M&A are outlined. As a second step, the chapter will more narrowly focus on the post-merger integration process and finally describes the problem at hand.

2.1 Mergers and Acquisitions – Basic Concepts

In order to fully understand the complex field of mergers and acquisitions, the following part describes basic concepts such as the development of M&A and its increasing importance during the last 30 years. It further outlines several types and processes of M&A. The section closes by outlining motives, as well as objectives of the M&A activities.

2.1.1 Importance and Development of M&A

M&A's are seen as a promising field of doing business. Through a M&A type transaction, a company can enter a market and use competence and local know-how without facing difficulties in establishing new subsidiaries (Teerikangas & Very, 2006, p. 31). M&A activities can be classified into several cyclical periods which are based on two opposing theories: neoclassical theory and behavioral theory (Harford, 2005, pp. 532-538). The latter argues that waves are shaped by the overvaluation of the market wherein "[...] managers use overvalued stock to buy the assets of lower-valued firms" (Depamphilis, 2010, p. 13). The neoclassical theory supports the argument, that M&A waves are the result of industrial shocks, such as a changing economic environment or new technologies and regulative restrictions respectively (Depamphilis, 2010, p. 13). Taking into consideration the time frame ranging from the year of 1895 until today, there are in total six waves of M&A activity (Jansen, 2008, p. 62). The exact dates of each wave vary from study to study (Depamphilis, 2010, pp. 16-18; Jansen, 2008, pp. 71-72; Gorzala, 2010, p. 5). The following part, however, outlines the waves relying on the dates defined by Jansen (Jansen, 2008, p. 63-72). Its characteristics are mainly based on the American market as only limited data or the European market was available until 1980. The part concludes by reflecting on the present M&A activities and the implications of the waves.

First wave: The first wave started with the recovery of the economic crisis in 1881 (Behringer, 2013, p. 31). The fast technological progress in the transportation sector, the news and production technique combined with a slow increase development of consumption functioned as a trigger for the first wave (Weston, Mitchell, & Mulherin, 2004, p. 40) which took place at the end of the 19th century (Becker, 2005, p. 8). This time period was a breeding ground for horizontal transactions whose main motivation consisted in establishing influencing monopolies (Depamphilis, 2012, p. 17; Weston et al., 2004, p. 172). Main objectives were the creation of a comparative advantage and the reduction of the price competitiveness (Behringer, 2013, p. 32). The creation of monopolies caused authorities to introduce counteractive measures such as the Sherman Antitrust Act in 1890 (Becker, 2005, p. 9) which aimed at restricting agreements within companies while allowing quasi-monopoly (Jansen, 2008, p. 63). Today's well known companies, like General Electric or American Tobacco, used the favorable environment (Behringer, 2013, p. 31). The first wave ended with the stock market crash in 1904 (Depamphilis, 2010, p. 17) and the Northern Securities Decision that influenced Section II of the Sherman Act, signed in 1904, and Clayton Antitrust Act, signed in 1914. (Becker, 2005, p. 8; Jansen, 2008, p. 63).

Second wave: Stricter cartel laws and the exhaustion of attractive conditions for monopolies forced companies to integrate vertically (Behringer, 2013, p. 32). Consequently an oligopolistic market structure (Jansen, 2008, p. 63) dominated the economy. Driving forces of the second wave, which took place between the years of 1916-1929, were the entry into the World War I (Depamphilis, 2010, p. 17), the increasing transportation systems system and the growing radio broadcasting which enhanced competition (Behringer, 2013, p. 32). The second wave collapsed with the stock market crash in 1929 (Depamphilis, 2010, p. 17).

Third wave: The third wave, which took place from 1965 to 1969, was characterized by a rising stock market, the economic boom (Depamphilis, 2010, p. 17) and an establishment of new company forms (Behringer, 2013, p. 33). The increasing activity by conglomerates arose with the portfolio theory and its ideas of risk diversification (Jansen, 2008, p. 63). Through an M&A transaction, companies saw their chance to expand into new geographical and industrial markets (Behringer, 2013, p. 36). The third wave had its peak in 1968 and found its end in 1969 with escalating purchase prices (Depamphilis, 2010, p. 17), the introduction of the Tax Reform Act, (Jansen, 2008, p. 64) and the oil crisis (Behringer, 2013, p. 36).

Fourth wave: The fourth wave, from 1984 to 1989, is seen as the most energetic one with respect to the degree of M&A activity (Jansen, 2008, p. 64). Most firms realized to concentrate on core competencies and consequently perceived conglomerate structures as inefficient (Behringer, 2013, p. 36). The fourth wave was driven by internationalization, disinvestments and liberalization of state owned companies (Jansen, 2008, p. 64). Forces like the economic boom, the favorable regulatory environment and beneficial foreign accounting practices supported the rise of hostile takeovers and corporate raiders (Behringer, 2013, p. 36). The relative amount of hostile takeover compared to the total amount of takeover was not significant. However, the value of the transactions conducted in a hostile manner was enormous (Gorzala, 2010, p. 5). The most spectacular transaction was the hostile takeover of RJR Nabisco, a tobacco and food producing company, through the acquirer Kohlberg Kravis Roberts & Co, a financial investor, with a transaction volume of 25 billion USD (Behringer, 2013, p. 37). Within this period, M&A transaction became more strategic and firms focused on synergy effects which enhanced the return on investment (ROI) (Jansen, 2001, p. 71). This period left collapsing conglomerates and junk bonds that were used to finance transaction (Depamphilis, 2010, p. 17). From 1985 onwards, M&A were used as transactions of finance (Jansen, 2001, p. 71). The fourth wave came to an end in 1989 and was followed by an economic slowdown (Gorzala, 2010, p. 5).

Fifth wave: The fifth wave, 1993-2000, started with a recovery of the M&A transactions. At an unexpected speed, this wave flooded the years of 1990s (Behringer, 2013, p. 37). Promoting factors such as globalization, the development of shareholder value and the speculative initial public offering (IPO) functioned as the main forces (Jansen, 2008, p. 65). Firms concentrated more on single business segments and horizontal acquisitions began to rise (Jansen, 2001, p. 71). As preferred sectors were the computer and telecommunication industry, the internet bubble is highly connected with the fifth wave (Behringer, 2013, p. 37). The amount of hostile takeovers decreased and merger of equals, like Daimler-Benz and Chrysler or Grand Met and Guinness dominated the market (Behringer, 2013, p. 37). Accompanied with the high volume of the average takeovers, share deals were preferred over cash deals: 80% of the deals having a transaction volume of more than 2 billion DM were financed through share deals (Jansen, 2008, pp. 65-67). Disinvestments and demergers have become a trend, as for example the demerger of BMW and Rover (Jansen, 2008, p. 68). As previously indicated, 16.5% of all transactions within the years of 1996 and 2000, were realized in industry sectors like computer and services. Due to the fact that those industries were seen overvalued, the transactions decreased from the year 2000 onwards until the next wave (Rhodes-Kropf & Viswanathan, 2004, p. 2685). Generally it is to be said that this fifth wave destroyed an incredible amount of value: Out of 4,136 transaction within the US, 87 takeovers destroyed a total value of 397 billion USD. The remaining 4,049 transactions produced value with a size of 157 billion USD. Consequently, the shareholders were left with a total loss of 240 billion USD (Behringer, 2013, p. 38).

Sixth wave: The sixth wave started in 2002 and ended in 2008/09. All of the worldwide transaction volumes from the previous waves were by far exceeded in year of 2006 (Jansen, 2008, p. 69). Despite the sub-prime crisis in 2007, transaction volumes, mainly forced by the first half of the year, increased by 20 % as compared to 2006 (Jansen, 2008, p. 69). Driving forces were the low interest rates, the rising stock market, a boom in the global economy, globalization and high commodity prices (Depamphilis, 2010, p. 16). In contrast to the fifth wave, medium sized companies dominated the M&A activities (Jansen, 2008, p. 72). The transaction volume decreased with the increasing financial crisis and its negative impacts on the economic environment (Jansen, 2008, pp. 69-71). Influencing individuals of the sixth wave were financial investors who took benefit from the expansive monetary policies introduced by the central banks (Behringer, 2013, p. 39). By the end of the wave, however, they had to pass on their power to governments and strategic investors (Kunisch, 2008, p. 48). The final end of the wave arose with the loss of confidence in global capital markets and the overall economic slowdown in industrial nations (Depamphilis, 2010, p. 17). Figure 1 provides an overview of mergers and acquisitions with respect to the value of transaction and number of transactions starting in 1985.

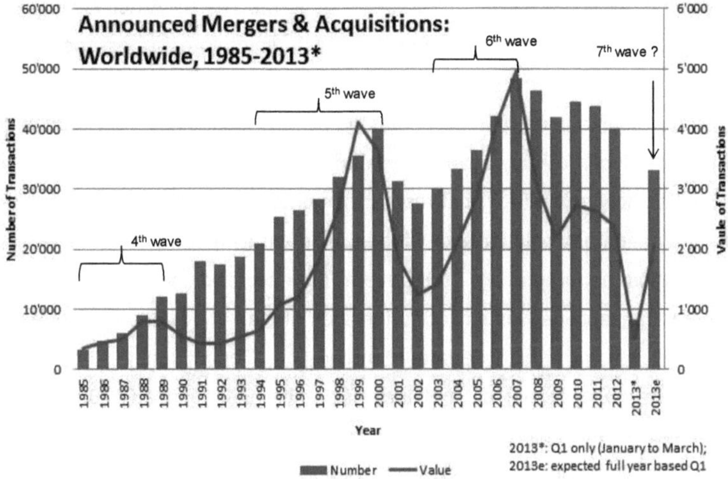

Figure 1 Announced M&A's Worldwide, 1985-2013
Adopted source from imaa (2013)

Present

After the recession, the question arises, when the world has to expect a next M&A wave. In fact, there is no clear answer. One the one hand, transaction volumes in 2012 have stagnated (Kary, 2013, p. 11). One the other hand, relying on the supportive economic factors at present, one could argue for a possible seventh M&A wave: Present M&A activity is expected to rise based on growing certainty about the U.S fiscal and tax policy and the improvement of the European debt crisis (Behringer, 2013, p. 29). This in turn fosters consumer confidence and the overall economic environment (Isom et al. 2013, p. 1). Furthermore, conditions like the low interest rate (e.g., interest rate ECB= 0.5%) (European Central Bank, 2013), the rising stock market (e.g., annual growth of DAX index = 31%) (Bloomberg, 2013), and the growing globalization are positive indicators for an increasing M&A activity. Another factor that should not be underestimated, are the present M&A topics catching the attention of the media.

Reports on, for example, the thrilling transaction activities of Walter Niemetz GmbH, raise public attention (Kary, 2013, p. 11).

Wave reflection

Reflecting on the waves, there are three concepts that need to be mentioned: First, all of the waves show similar patterns. The M&A activity was promoted by external factors like economic growth, low interest rates and a rising stock market. From a historical perspective, each way differs according to industrial development which is accompanied by new technology, new regulations and different types of transaction (Depamphilis, 2010, p. 16). Secondly, only a few waves show a need for post-merger competence, as vertical and conglomerate integration ask only for a low degree of integration. Financial transactions require almost no integration. Furthermore, the integration competence in early horizontal transactions was limited to the area of market power, which does not necessarily ask for a high degree of integration. Consequently, the need for post-merger management did not increase until 1990 (Jansen, 2001, p. 71). Duchin and Schmid (2013), raise the third aspect which refers to different M&A management behavior during M&A waves (Duchin & Schmid, 2013, p. 84). Interestingly, mergers conducted within a merger wave show less quality and more uncertainty as compared to mergers realized outside a wave. They also found that managers who were responsible for in-wave mergers had to face less termination as compared to the out-wave acquiring firms (Duchin & Schmid, 2013, p. 84).

2.1.2 Types of Strategic Combinations

The term M&A itself is used in literature in a broad sense. It includes all strategic combinations of firms ranging from a collaboration of companies to complex acquisitions of firms (Balz & Arlinghaus, 2007, p. 12; Bauer & Matzler, Developing a better measure for speed of integration, 2012). Marks and Mirvis (2010) categorize the forms of combination according to their degree of commitment and the level of investment between the merging firms (Marks & Mirvis, 2010, p. 12). Figure 2 illustrates the types of strategic combinations followed by a rough description of each single one.

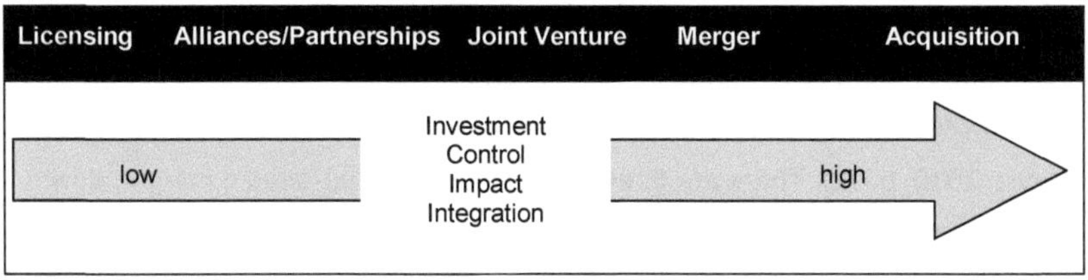

Figure 2 Strategic Combinations
Own elaboration according to Marks & Mrivis (2010), p. 12

Licensing: The first type of strategic combination that is situated at the lower level of the scale requires a relatively low commitment and is the simplest form as compared to the other combinations. According to Bell (1996), "licensing agreements are long-term contracts which cover the transfer of the right to use a specific know-how" (Bell, 1996, p. 11). Many firms engage in licensing as it provides access to difficult or risky markets and provides low capital risk and low commitment of resources. However, this might lead to a creation of possible competitors and a limitation of control (Bradley, 2005, p. 244). A special form of licensing is franchising. Within the system of franchising, business partners engage in a cooperative, long-term and contractual agreement which limits the right holder in its freedom of doing business (Meffert, Burmann, & Kirchgeorg, 2008, p. 587).

Alliances and partnerships: Alliances and partnerships consist of two or more firms who show a mutual need that is to compete in international markets with the help of exchanging assets (Bradley, 2005, p. 241). A firm benefits in engaging in an alliance as this form of strategic combination provides access to assets, technology, products and markets that have been not available so far. Consequently, synergy effects are achieved (Bradley, 2005, pp. 240-241).

Joint ventures: Joint ventures differ from the alliances and partnership in several characteristics. "A joint venture goes further, by establishing a complete and separate formal organization with its own structure, governance, workforce, procedures, policies and culture – while the predecessor companies still exist" (Marks & Mirvis, 2010, p. 12). Joint ventures facilitate the transfer of technology and reduce risk when entering an international environment (Bradley, 2005, p. 249). However, disadvantages arise with the cost of control and the creation of a potential competitor (Bradley, 2005, p. 253).

Merger: Another strategic combination, which is situated almost at the very end of the scale, represented in Figure 1, is the merger. Choosing this type, two completely separated companies agree to form a new entity (Marks & Mirvis, 2010, p. 12). There are three types of mergers: up-stream merger, down-stream mergers and side-stream merger. The latter one describes an integration of two firms that are based on the same levels. An up-stream merger integrates the subsidiary into the parent firm. If that parent firm is integrated into the subsidiary, one speaks of a so called down-stream merger (Brähler, 2008, p. 227).

Acquisitions: The strategic combination that requires the highest degree of commitment, integration, investment, control and pain of separation is represented by the acquisition (see Figure 2). Within an acquisition the buyer company purchases an organization for incorporation into its firm (Marks & Mirvis, 2010, p. 12). An acquisition may be realized through an asset deal or a share deal. The latter one describes the purchase of shares whereas the first one represents the purchase of assets or goods (Jansen, 2008, p. 247).

For the purpose of this study the term M&A shall be used in a strict sense, that is only the terms merger and acquisitions are considered without integrating the remaining types of strategic combinations.

2.1.3 Categorization of M&A

Generally, the types of M&A transactions are classified according to the strategic or financial perspective, the technique oriented approach and the corporate culture. Table 2 represents the different categories and types of M&A:

Types of M&A		
Strategy Perspective	**Corporate Structure Perspective**	**Technique Perspective**
• Horizontal • Vertical • Conglomerate	• Acquisition • Consolidation	• Hostile • Friendly

Table 2 Types of M&A
Own elaboration according to Sharan (2003), pp. 32-33

Strategy Perspective: Based on the strategic perspective, integration can be conducted horizontally, vertically or as a conglomerate. A horizontal M&A (e.g., Daimler-Benz and Chrysler merger) is a business consolidation of two firms who are active in similar fields, often offering the same goods or services (Sharan, 2003, p. 32) and having a competitive relationship (Weston, Mitchell, & Mulherin, 2004, pp. 7-8) Due to its beneficial size, the creation of economies of scale is facilitated (Sharan, 2003, p. 32). Integration among firms operating in different stages of the production process concerning one single product is called vertical integration (Weston et al., 2004, pp. 7-8). Most firms choose this type of transactions as it reduces costs of communication and transportation. It furthermore simplifies the coordination of products and the input supply (Sharan, 2003, p. 32). A third type of merger is the so called conglomerate in which at least two firms decide to merge without being active in the same field of business (Weston et al., 2004, p. 7). A conglomerate can emerge through product extension or geographic market extension. There is also the possibility of a pure conglomerate merger including a financial conglomerate or managerial conglomerate in which the respective function is combined under one roof (Sharan, 2003, p. 32).

Corporate Structure Perspective: Sharan (2013) distinguishes between the acquisition and consolidation, also called amalgamation. The latter describes the process wherein two firms combine their two identities into one new identity (Sharan, 2003, p. 32). An acquisition, as described in section 2.1.1, consists of the acquiring firm and the target firm maintaining one firm without creating a new entity (Sharan, 2003, p. 32).

Technique Perspective: From the perspective of the M&A technique, a transaction can be either hostile or friendly. The latter one describes a takeover process by purchasing shares in relatively short time frame which can occur either as a dawn raid or an irrevocable call option (Sharan, 2003, pp. 32-33). The relative number of hostile takeovers has decreased from 10.9% in 2008 to 2.4% in 2012 (Mergermarket, Statista, 2013). Firms have various choices in fighting against the unwanted takeover (Becker, 2005, p. 67). They have the possibility to choose among pre-bid defenses, including among others poison pill and super-majority provisions, and post-bid defenses, like for example greenmail, standstill agreement or asset restructuring (Gorzala, 2010, pp. 12-18). Contradicting the hostile takeover, a friendly takeover is characterized by various negotiations. The process is relatively secure as the participants agree and later sign the confidentiality letter and letter of intent respectively (Sharan, 2003, p. 34).

2.1.4 M&A Process

Depending on the studies and research approaches, there are various categorizations and viewpoints when it comes to the M&A process, ranging from two to ten phases (Calipha, Tarba, & Brock, 2010, p. 5). Boland (1970) roughly divides the M&A process into post-merger and pre-merger phase (Boland, 1970, pp. 8-11), whereas Schweiger and Weber (1989) summarize the M&A process with pre-merger phase and implementation phase (Schweiger & Weber, 1989, pp. 69-86). Picot (2000) narrows the M&A process and defines three phases: planning, transaction and integration (Picot, 2000, p. 8). The phase model of Jansen (2008) is also subdivided into three stages: strategically phase of analysis and conception, transaction phase and integration phase (Jansen, 2008, p. 249). Similarly, a three phase integration is suggested by Marks and Mirvis (2010): Pre-combination, combination and post-combination phase (Marks & Mirvis, 2010, pp. 3-15). DePamphilis argues for a more detailed approach and introduces the merger and acquisition process consisting of ten phases (Depamphilis, 2010, pp. 129-135). No matter if the M&A process is sub-divided into two or ten phases, the principle pattern is similar: Analyzing how M&As set their objective, choose a partner, prepare to merge, integrate different processes, handle culture and develop a sustainable environment (Calipha, Tarba, & Brock, 2010, p. 7). As the M&A process is a complex phenomenon, one has to consider the whole picture. With a development of M&A research, there is an increasing group of experts who recommend focusing on a more holistic approach (e.g., Bauer & Matzler, 2013, p.5; Calipha, 2010, p.7) and treating the overall deal as a lifecycle (Chanmugam, Shill, Mann, Ficery, & Pursche, 2005). The outlined numbers of stages show a variety of possibilities to categorize the M&A process. In general, the phases can be summarized as pre-merger phase, transaction phase and post-merger phase (see Figure 3).

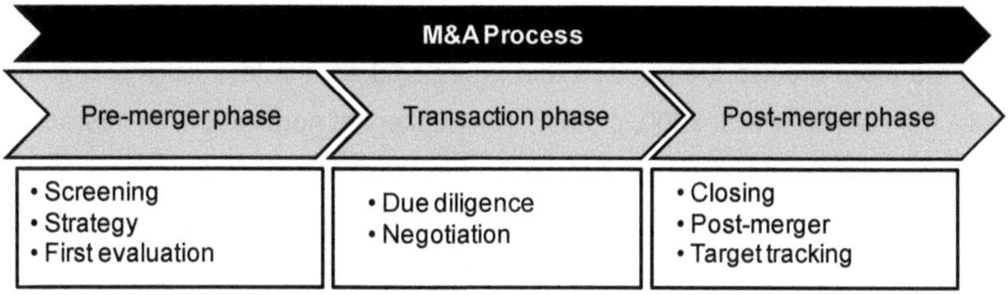

Figure 3 M&A Process
Own elaboration according to Jansen (2008), p. 249 and Picot (2000), p. 21

Pre-merger integration: The first step of an M&A process is the pre-merger phase which starts with an analysis and study of the buyer firm itself, that is analyzing its own goals as well as strategic potential and limitations (Jansen, 2008, p. 249). Once the buyer company has strategically decided to realize an M&A activity, the buyer company develops a process plan including considerations of business administration and tax law (Picot, 2000, p. 21). The firm is well advised to integrate external and internal groups of the M&A process from the beginning onwards. The latter one consists for example of the owner of acquiring firm, the top management, operational management, professional M&A groups. External members might be certified accountant, customer, supplier and governmental institutions (Voss & Müller-Stewens, 2006, pp. 29-40). As a next step the buyer firm screens all potential companies based on the criteria that has been set in the strategic plan (Voss & Müller-Stewens, 2006, p. 13). Within the process of screening, the buyer company analyzes and forecasts the competitive environment (Picot, 2000, p. 16). Having successfully analyzed and chosen the right firm, the buyer company can now step into the next phase.

Transaction phase: The phase of transaction combines two significant parts of the M&A process: Due diligence and negotiation. In order to clarify the scope and the value of the company in a relativly early stage of negotiations, due diligence provides the perfect tool (Depamphilis, 2010, p. 182; Picot, 2000, p. 95). A due diligence review is made throughout all fields within the company, ranging from financial, marketing, HR, legal, and tax as well as environmental and organizational due diligence (Jansen, 2008, p. 276). With the help of a due diligence review the buyer company aims to eliminate the risk of the transaction.

Consequently, the more detailed the information given in a due diligence review and the more precise the process that is undertaken, the less risky seems the M&A transaction (Pack, 2000, p. 251). The concept of negotiation, an interactive process, plays a decisive role throughout the transaction process. It accompanies the whole due diligence process and finally defines the actual purchase price of the acquired business (Depamphilis, 2010, p. 175). Therefore, it turns out to be crucial to have a well-developed negotiation strategy with well-informed negotiators who defend the interests of the company.

Post-merger integration: The two previous phases form the basis for the third and most important one: The post-merger integration. Success or failure of the overall M&A transaction is determined in phase of integration as it is decisive for value creation and synergy realization (Haspeslagh & Jemison, 1991, p. 23). Jansen (2008) suggests three steps in order to successfully integrate: Post-merger planning (i.e., analysis of integration potential), the interconnection of six levels (i.e., organizational, strategic, administrative, operative, cultural and external integration) and finally the performance review (i.e., review on economic efficiency, realization of synergies, costs of integration and creation of a balance score card) (Jansen, 2008, p. 241). The post-merger integration is a central issue within the paper. Therefore, an extended and detailed description of the value creating process is given in part 2.2 of the paper.

Risk: As mentioned previously in this chapter, M&A managers have to handle and face the risk that arises with the M&A process. Interestingly, the degree of risk differs among the three phases (Habeck, Kröger, & Träm, 2002, p. 15). According to a study on top management, only 17% of the respondents evaluate the transaction phase as risky whereas the pre-merger phase with its screening processes and evaluation of the appropriate company is perceived more risky, that is 30%. The most uncertain and therefore most risky phase is the post-merger integration. More than half (i.e. 53%) of top management sees the integration phase as risky (Habeck et al., 2002, p. 16). Those numbers show an enormous need for research with respect to the post-merger integration. The paper therefore focuses on the third phase of integration and provides a deeper insight into to integration phase in part 2.2.

2.1.5 Motives and Objectives of M&A

Although M&A is a relatively risky type of entry mode (Marks & Mirvis, 2010, p. 12), firms still do engage in a M&A transactions. But why are they still driven to merge and which motives support their decision? Generally, motives can be divided into value maximizing or financial motives and non-value maximizing or managerial motives (Cartwright, 2005, p. 6). While the latter one refers to managerial pride and market power, value maximizing motives aim at financial and operating synergies (Cartwright, 2005, p. 6). Table 3 provides an overview of the more prominent theories that have been developed in M&A literature so far. While some of them are clear financial or managerial oriented motives, others tend to be a combination of both.

M&A Motives		
	Theory	Motivation
Value maximizing motives	**Operating synergy**	Improve operating efficiency through economies of scale and economies of scope by acquiring a customer, supplier, or competitor
	Financial synergy	Lower cost of capital
	Tax considerations	Obtain unused net operating losses and tax credits, asset write-ups, and substitute capital gains for ordinary income
Combination	**Market power / Collusive synergy**	Improve monopoly power: Increase market share to improve ability to set prices above competitive level
	Diversification	Position the firm in a higher-growth products or markets by using three diversification options: New products in current markets; new products in new markets; or current products in new markets
	Buying undervalued assets	Acquire assets cheaper when the equity of existing companies is less than the cost of buying or building assets
Non- value maximizing motives	**Strategic realignment**	Acquire capabilities to adapt more rapidly to environmental changes than could be achieved if developed internally. Change occurs mainly from technological chance and regulatory or political change
	Mismanagement	Merger correct the agency problem (i.e., the separation between managers interests and owners goals)
	Managerialism	Managers acquire companies for selfish reason: Increase size of company and management power
	Hubris (managerial pride)	Acquirers believe that their own target valuation is superior to the market's valuation → Overpayment by overestimating synergy
	Misvaluation	Investor overvaluation of acquirer's stock encourages M&A

Table 3 M&A Motives
Own elaboration according to DePamphilis (2010), p. 6 and Sharan (2003), p.41

While the table provides different areas of motives, Angwin (2007) argues that M&A activities are driven by a combination of those motives and that the real reasons behind the motivation have to be taken into consideration (Angwin D. , 2007, pp. 101-102). Christensen and colleagues (2011) summarize and conclude that managers are motivated by basically two factors: improving the current performance and reinventing a business model (Christensen, Alton, Rising, & Waldeck, 2011, p. 50). A more practical wrap-up is given by Nahass and colleagues: "While there may be many reasons for pursuing a merger or acquisition, it's ultimately about creating long-term value for shareholders. That's what doing business—and deals—is all about" (Nahass, Boyle, Smith, Balog, Kennedy, & Skorupka, 2008, p. 3). Knowing the motives, it is however of importance to reflect on the time aspect as motives may change over time. In contrast to the goals of the 1980's, a driving force in the 1990s, for example, was to fight for the strategic position in industries as a result of globalization (Teerikangas & Very, 2006, p. 40). Today, other motivations play an important role. According to a study conducted by Isom and colleagues (2013) the present motives encompass issues like companies geographic reach (20%), profitable operations from the perspective of financial buyer (19%), entering into a new line of business (17%), expanding customer base (15%) (Isom et al., 2013, p. 3). Additionally, there are changing managerial approaches due to M&A research and experience (Teerikangas & Very, 2006, p. 40).

According to a study conducted by Walter (1990), it is not possible to generalize all of the objectives of a M&A transaction. He argues therefore that different objectives can be categorized according to its importance and the type of transaction (Walter & Barney, 1990, p. 79). Managing resource dependence, for example, is of particular importance for vertical transactions. As horizontal M&A reach various objectives simultaneously, they are not particularly dominated by an objective. Finally, the utilization of financial capability and the entering into new business dominate the goal setting of conglomerate (Walter & Barney, 1990, p. 84).

2.1.6 Four Schools of Thought

M&A research has been conducted for about 50 years now (Cartwright, 2005, p. 1). However, the research itself differs in terms of its methods and research areas (Capasso & Meglio, 2005, p. 201; Cartwright & Schoenberg, 2006, p. 2). With the increasing M&A literature, several theories dominted the M&A research such as free cash flow, efficient market hypothesis, indutrial organization economics, resource based view of the firms, acculturaltion theory and behavioral theory of the firm (Birkinshaw, Bresman, & Hakanson, 2000, p. 397). In order to structure those conceptual assumptions and classify the indiviudal approaches, four schools of thought have been developed (Haspeslagh & Jemison, 1991, pp. 292-309) The four schools of thought differ in terms of their objectives, theoretical underpinnings and central hypotheses (see Table 3).

Four Schools of Thought			
Research stream	**Objective function**	**Theoretical underpinnings**	**Central proposition for each theoretical aspect**
Financial Economics	Value creation for shareholders and economy as a whole	Market corporate control; free cash flow; efficient market hypothesis; agency theory; capital asset pricing model	Acquisitions enhance the efficiency of the market for corporate control → net wealth gain for shareholders
Strategic Management	Performance of buyer and target company	Industrial organization economics	Realization of synergies positively impact the acquirer performance
		Resource based view of the firm	Only unique synergies or unexpected synergies will have a positive impact on acquirer performance
Organizational Behavior	Impact of acquisition on individuals and organization culture	Acculturation Theory	Employee satisfaction and effective integration is facilitated through congruent cultures of merging firms
Process Perspective	Creation of value after the acquisition	Behavioral theory of the firm	The actions of management and the process of integration determines the extent to which the potential of the acquisition are realized

Table 4 Overview Four Schools of Thought
Own elaboration according to Birkinshaw et al. (2000), p. 397 and Haspeslagh & Jemison (1991), pp. 292-309

Table 3 provides evidence for the fact that M&A research has been specialized in diverse directions. The following section outlines roughly the financial economics school and strategic management school. A more comprehensive view is taken on the organizational behavior school as well as the process perspective school, as they form the basis for the two central types of integration analyzed in my study.

Financial Economics School

The central question within the financial economics theory, also called the capital markets school, is whether M&A transactions create financial value (Haspeslagh & Jemison, 1991, p. 293). The main objective of this field of research is to explore the interdependence of corporate control and shareholder value (Datta, 1991, p. 282). Within this stream, the shareholder value represents the central goal that needs to be maximized (Birkinshaw, Bresman, & Hakanson, 2000, p. 397). In order to explore the factors that lead to value creation, the movements of the capital markets after the transactions are analyzed (Haspeslagh & Jemison, 1991, p. 293). Those reactions are observed within a given period of time (Becker, 2005, p. 89; Haspeslagh & Jemison, 1991, p. 295), ranging from the date of announcement to the post-merger phase (Becker, 2005, p. 81). If the net change of the market value is positive, the financial economics theory assumes that wealth has been created for the shareholders (Haspeslagh & Jemison, 1991, p. 295). Generally, the most dramatic changes of the share prices are expected within the time of announcement of the deal (Jensen & Ruback, 1983, pp. 9-15), as the uncertainty and speculations are assumed to be the highest. Apparent from Table 4, several theories support the financial economics school of thought. For the purpose of the paper, only a view are presented within the following lines. Some financial economist based their view, for example, on the agency theory, wherein managers functions as agents of shareholders and might differ in their interests (Haspeslagh & Jemison, 1991, p. 294). Another underpinning arises from the free cash flow where the economists assume that managers would return the free cash flow to their shareholder in situation like a M&A transaction (Haspeslagh & Jemison, 1991, p. 294). Studies that are conducted on the basis of capital markets are driven by essentially three models which encompass the capital asset pricing model, the market model and the average excess return model (Becker, 2005, p. 86; Singh & Montgomery, 1987, pp. 380-382). At this point the models are not explained in detail as it would go beyond the actual content of the paper. Summarizing the financial school of thought, it is still questionable whether transactions have a positive financial effect for the buyer company (Meyer, 2008, p. 197). Furthermore, this school of thought ignores additional factors that might influence the share price development (Buono & Bowditch, 2003, p. 10).

Strategic Management School

In contrast to the financial economics school, the strategic management school concentrates on long-term value creation at the individual company level that is realized through competitive advantage (Birkinshaw et al., 2000, p. 397; Schmidt, Vogt, & Schriber, 2005, p. 306). As the different M&A phases interact with each other, the strategic management school investigates the whole M&A process, ranging from the pre-merger phase to the post-merger phase (Birkinshaw et al., 2000, p. 397). Scientists argue that despite the importance of the pre-merger phase, actual value is created in the post-merger phase (Jansen, 2008, p. 318; Haspelagh & Jemison, 1991, p. 103). The strategic management school is subdivided into two types of groups: the acquisition performance group and the acquisition planning group (Haspeslagh & Jemison, 1991, p. 300). The former one empirically develops the probability of M&A success with respect to various characteristics of the companies concerned. The probable success rate is then compared with the actual measured success (Haspelagh & Jemison, 1991, p. 301). Empirically analyzed are areas like relative size, market share and pre-acquisition experience (Birkinshaw, 2000, p. 397). Based on the finding of the acquisition performance group, the acquisition planning group develops strategic concepts to increase the M&A performance (Haspeslagh & Jemison, 1991, p.303).

Organizational Behavior School

The organizational behavior school reflects on behavioral aspects in terms of M&A process, that is the individual person engaged in a M&A activity (Haspeslagh & Jemison, 1991, p. 303). In course of research, it became obvious that the increasing negative behavior of individuals in connection with M&A activities is the result of ignoring the influence of human and cultural integration within the M&A process (Capasso & Meglio, 2005, p. 202). Topics like merger stress, uncertainty or cultural clash gained attention throughout M&A research (Marks, 1997, p. 268; Seo & Hill, 2005, p. 425; Weber & Camerer, 2003, p. 401). Haspeslagh & Jemison (1991) categorzied the complex field of organization behavior theory into three areas. The first one enompasses human resources, while the second one is concerned with crisis literatur. The third area comprises organizational and cultural fit as well as compatibility (Haspelagh & Jemison, 1991, p. 304). Additionally, first studies started to examine the integration and acculturation process as essential topics of M&A activity. The following part provides an overview of the fields of organizational school wherein HR and crisis literature form the first part, followed by cultural compatibility and closing with the concept of acculturation and integration.

Influence of HR on M&A Performance and Crisis Literature

Individuals involved in a transaction process face enormous changes. As the cultural and human aspects influence the overall M&A process, those research areas are explored in literature of pre-merger integration as well as post-merger integration (Haspeslagh & Jemison, 1991, p.). Especially the integration process in the post-merger phase is concerned with the human factors of M&A activities (Larsson & Finkelstein, 1991, p. 2). In this phase, employees might face physical health problems (Marks, 1997, p. 268) as well as psychological pressure (Beth-von der Warth, 2004, p. 14). In order to circumvent those negative outcomes HR literature contributes to the M&A research in the fields of communication, trust, and the meaning of the overall human resource development (Bijlsma-Frankema, 2001, p. 199).

Cultural Compatibility

This subcategory of organizational behavior school is concerned with the concept of culture. As the term culture will be explicitly analyzed in section 2.2.2, only main issues are explained at this point. Generally, culture plays an increasing important role in M&A practice and M&A science (Shrivastava, 1986, p. 65). As culture is such a complex field of research, it poses problems in M&A activity. The integration of two different cultures challenges almost every M&A transaction and increases the risk to fail (Buono & Bowditch, 2003, p. 16). Consequqenlty, a lack of cultural fit is assumed to show a negative M&A

perfomance as uncertainty of employees increases (Bijlsma-Frankema, 2001, p. 192; Kavanagh & Askanasy, 2006, p. 84). In contrast, a positive cultural fit may enhance synergy realization within the post-merger integration (Chatterjee, Lubatkin, Schweiger, & Weber, 1992, p. 320). It seems rational that similar cultures enhance cultural compatibility. However, cultural difference may to some extent positively contribute to a cultural fit and therefore to the overall M&A performance (Teerikangas & Very, 2006, p. 32). Analyzing the impact on M&A performance with respect to culture, researchers also make use of the concept organizational fit which evolves over time (Kavanagh & Askanasy, 2006, p. 84) and encompasses additionally personnel and administrative issues (Kenneth & Harbir, 1994, p. 253).

Integration and Acculturation

A third theoretical underpinning within the organizational behavior school is the concept integration in connection with the process of acculturation. Is has to be stated, that those two concepts are also studied within the process school of thought (Birkinshaw et al., p. 380; Haspeslagh & Jemison, 1991, p. 309). As process school is based on the organizational behavior school (Haspeslagh & Jemison, 1991, p. 309), it is obvious that some fields of research might overlap. The integration takes place within the post-merger phase wherein goals, which have been defined in the pre-merger phase, are supposed to be realized (Glaum & Hutzschenreuter, 2010, p. 210). General success factors range from the ability of human integration (e.g. Shrivastava, 1986, p. 65), the degree of integration (Haspelagh & Jemison, 1991, p. 33) and the speed of integration (e.g. Angwin, 2004, p. 218). The latter two concepts mainly find their application within the process school of thought, which will be described thereafter.

The acculturation theory describes the process of combining two organizational cultures in course of the integration process (Nahavandi & Malekzadeh, 1988 , p. 82). Nahavandi and Malekzadeh (1988) describe the possible integration processes depending on the perception of the attractiveness of the buyer firm and the willingness of the acquired company to preserve its own culture (Nahavandi & Malekzadeh, 1988 , p. 83). The four modes of acculturation are respresemted in Figure 4.

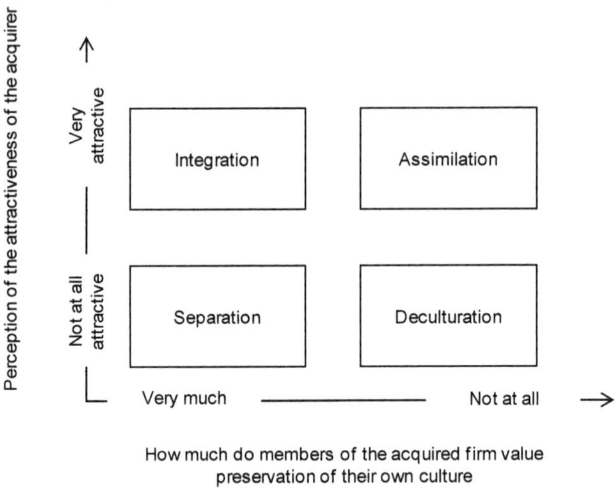

Figure 4 Modes of Acculturation
Own illustration according to Nahavandi & Malekzadeh (1988), p. 83

Within the model of acculturation, integration describes the willingness of the acquired company to keep their own culture while perceiving the buyer company as very attractive (Nahavandi & Malekzadeh, 1988, p. 82). The meaning of the term integration in connection to acculturation is to be strictly separated from the overall meaning within the paper. The latter one describes the overall phase of post-merger integration. Within the process of assimilation, integration describes the process wherein the target company accepts the culture of the buyer company while its own culture is not as attractive. Consequently a cultural identity will occur (Nahavandi & Malekzadeh, 1988, p. 82). The urgent need of preserving one's own culture combined with a negative perception of the buyer's culture results into a so called separation. The acquired firms will more or less live its own life and function independently (Nahavandi & Malekzadeh, 1988, p. 82). A complete alienation with one's own culture and the culture of the buyer company is represented in the fourth mode of acculturation (Nahavandi & Malekzadeh, 1988, p. 83). To conclude, it shows that various tendencies have been made towards employee satisfaction and effective integration. I will return to this important field of research in section 2.2.2, as the assumptions of the paper builds on aspects of human integration.

Process Perspective School

The process perspective school is built on the two previous strategic management schools of thought (i.e., management school of thought and organizational behavior school of thought) and combines the ideas developed within those areas (Haspeslagh & Jemison, 1991, p. 306). This school of thought focuses on the management activities realized within the post-merger integration (Birkinshaw et al., 2000, p. 398) wherein this integration process itself is seen as an influential factor on M&A succes (Haspeslagh & Jemison, 1991, p. 306; Stahl & Voight, 2006, p. 162). A special focus lies within the speed of integration, as it seems to affect the M&A performance (Puranam, Singh, & Chaudhuri, 2009, p. 183). A more in depth analysis of the post-merger integration and its implications on M&A perfomance will be provided in part 2.2. In summary, this theory provides practical advises for managers operating in the integration process and shows determining factors influencing the integration process (Cartwright, 2005, p. 2; Schlüzen & Jöns, 2003, p. 3).

For the purpose of the paper, particular attention is given to the process perspective school and organizational behavior school as they include task integration and human integration respectively (Birkinshaw, Bresman, & Hakanson, 2000, p. 399).

2.2 M&A Post-Merger Integration

Largely neglected by the financial economics and strategic management school of thought is the concept of post-merger integration. However, studies of the organizational behavior and process perspective emphasize the importance of post-merger integration. In fact, it is a critical factor for the overall M&A performance (Stahl & Voigt, 2008, p. 162). The following part first of all outlines the integration concept in general. Subsequently, main attention is drawn on the three concepts that will play a decisive role when it comes to model and hypothesis development: Human and task integration as well as speed of integration.

2.2.1 Degree of Integration and General Arguments

M&A integration takes place in the post-merger phase and is the decisive factor for the M&A performance (Birkinshaw, Bresman, & Hakanson, 2000, p.

395; Stahl & Voigt, 2008, p. 162). Epstein (2004) defines the post merger integration as "a multi-faceted process that requires simultaneous efforts in various areas" (Epstein, 2004, p. 175). The complex integration process aims at value creation, which is achieved through actions initiated by managers, understanding those actions and its impacts and finally being able to communicate this process to all of the individuals involved in the M&A transaction (Birkinshaw et al. 2000, p. 395). Especially resource sharing and knowledge transfer is perceived as value creating factors (Cartwright & Schoenberg, 2006, p. 2).The significance of the integration process is proven in various M&A literature: Pablo (1994) argues, that the high failure rate of M&A is the result of mismanaged integration (Pablo, 1994, p. 804). Cartwright (2005) warns against the mistake to solely concentrate on the input and output of the M&A process, while ignoring the integration process itself (Cartwright, 2005, p. 2). In other words: The integration process is perceived as a black box (Stahl & Voigt, 2008, p. 172). It is therefore of high relevance to analyze the processes within this black box.

Degree of Integration

The question to which degree two companies should merge is a very complex one. The degree of integration, as a dimension of the post-merger phase, represents an indicator for organizational change and the resulting problems (Homburg & Bucerius, 2005, pp. 95-113; Larsson & Finkelstein, 1999, pp. 1-26). A company's degree of integration may range from no harmonization at all to complete integration (Bauer, 2012, p. 130). For several years now, M&A literature has discussed the relation of the degree of integration and the M&A performance. Despite different results, researchers agree to the fact that M&A performance and the degree of integration show a certain interrelation (Birkinshaw et al., 2000, p. 399; Colombo, Conca, Buongiorno, & Gnan, 2007, p. 203; Cording, Christman & King, 2008, p. 757; Homburg & Bucerius, 2005, p. 104; Larsson & Finkelstein, 1999, p. 6). The post-merger integration is shaped and may be categorized by the modes of integration (Wirtz, 2012, p. 308). Haspeslagh and Jemison (1991) argue that a company, depending on its strategic interdependency and its organizational autonomy, may define four categories of integration which are holding, absorption, preservation and symbiosis (Haspeslagh & Jemison, 1991, p. 145) (see Figure 5):

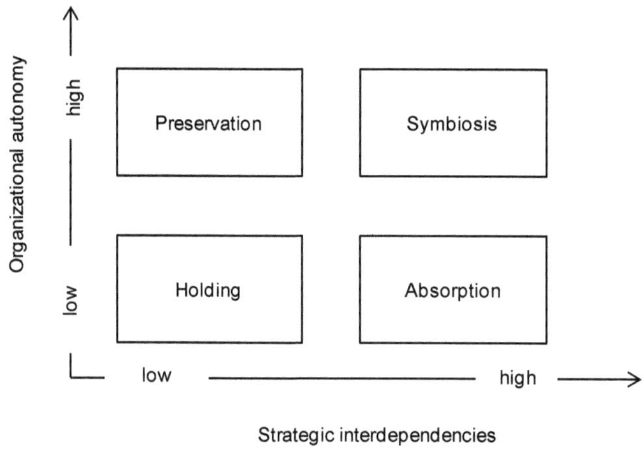

Figure 5 Modes of Integration
Own elaboration according to Haspeslagh & Jemison (1991), p. 145

Holding: A firm following the mode of holding aims at marginal or no integration at all. Value creation only takes place through activities like capital transfer, risk diversification, or general management capabilities that lead to optimization (Haspeslagh & Jemison, 1991, p. 146). This process asks for an integrated system of planning, control and information (Jansen, 2008, p. 327). In most of the cases, both firms are active in similar business areas (Haspeslagh & Jemison, 1991, p. 147).

Absorption: Merging companies engaging in absorption show a high degree of interdependency in order to reach the goal of value creation (Haspeslagh & Jemison, 1991, p. 147). Furthermore, for the given level of interdependency, only a minimum amount of organizational autonomy is necessary. The integration process is defined through full consolidation of activities and a full integration of the organizations and their culture (Haspeslagh & Jemison, 1991, p. 148). As a result, there are no borders anymore which of course demands time (Haspeslagh & Jemison, 1991, p. 148). This process is seen as the most complicated and time intense approach of integration (Jansen, 2008, p. 328).

Preservation: Within the mode of preservation, the buyer company aims at maintaining their organizational autonomy which requires only few strategic interdependencies among the companies (Haspeslagh & Jemison, 1991, p. 148). The buyer company is well advised to keep the source of the transferred advantages, and see the acquired company as an additional source of resources like for example capital (Haspeslagh & Jemison, 1991, p. 149). Value is created through risk taking, commitment, promotion of the acquired company and the learning process of the buyer company (Haspeslagh & Jemison, 1991, p. 149). A successful integration can only be achieved if the acquired company continues to work independently from the buyer company (Jansen, 2008, p. 327).

Symbiosis: The fourth mode of integration, symbiosis, represents a combination of a high degree of organizational autonomy and a high degree of strategic interdependencies. The later one requires a high transfer of capabilities (Haspeslagh & Jemison, 1991, p. 148). Within the organizational autonomy the transferred capabilities need to be preserved in an organizational context. Within this partial integration both companies maintain their boundaries in terms of identity and character and at the same time its permeability in terms of functional and management activities (Haspeslagh & Jemison, 1991, p. 148). In order to realize a complete symbiotic integration, each company has to acquire the others characteristics (Haspeslagh & Jemison, 1991, p. 150).

The integration processes can also be categorized according to its organizational levels. Shrivastava (1986) outlines three levels of integration, which consist of social cultural integration, also called human integration, procedural integration and physical integration. (Shrivastava, 1986, p. 68). The latter two can be summarized as task integration (Bauer, 2012, p. 130). Despite the categorization of the different integration levels, they are not mutually exclusive and have to be considered as interdependent systems that significantly influence the M&A performance (Birkinshaw et al., 2000, p. 396). Those interdependencies will be explained in more detail in part 3.1. For the purpose of the paper, human integration and task integration are analyzed in the following two sections.

2.2.2 Human Integration

The human integration process, here also referred cultural integration process or socio-cultural integration process, has become increasingly important in M&A literature. Some researches even go so far and state that cultural integration is the most critical type of integration as it involves combining cultures and managerial objectives (Shrivastava, 1986, p. 65). A recent study conducted by Isom and colleagues (2013) implies that 38% of the managers value cultural issues as the most significant aspect of integration (Isom, et al., 2013, p. 5). As the human integration process involves the interaction of individuals, it is strongly based on the cultures of the two merging firms. Therefore, the following part outlines the concept of culture itself and its impact on the integration process. As the human integration process is accompanied by challenges and chances, essential aspects such as merger stress, us-versus-them, trust and communication are explained.

Culture

The phenomenon of culture has gained more and more influence during the last couple of years within M&A research. As culture affects the daily business within the company, it becomes essential to integrate different cultures in order to productively maintain a newly formed organizational structure (Bijlsma-Frankema, 2001, p. 198). The different values, norms and attitudes within the different cultures form an obstacle for members in a merged culture to see things similar (Weber & Camerer, 2003, p. 401). For an increasing number of firms involved in an M&A activity, the awareness of culture has risen tremendously and it has become an attractive asset which improves efficiency and in which it is worth to invest (Hermalin, 2001, p. 218). For managers, it is quite challenge to successfully fulfill this task. It is therefore decisive to know the concept of culture itself. The majority of M&A literature focuses on two types of culture that are national and organizational culture. For the purpose of the paper, all of the statements and assumptions rely on the latter one: organizational culture. The concept of organizational culture was first introduced in the early 1980's (Teerikangas & Very, 2006, p. 32) and has in the course of time focused on different variables and its effects on M&A performance, as for example cultural fit (Larsson & Finkelstein, 1999). Bijlsma-Frankema (2001) captures the concept of organizational culture as follows: "Cultures in organizations are about the way members make sense of their experiences in the organization, the way they define and interpret the situations they are in, in order to be able to act in a meaningful way" (Bijlsma-Frankema, 2001, p. 194). This view is extended by Teerikangas and Very (2006) who characterize organizational culture as a secondary socialization process that is based on the primary socialization process, or national culture respectively (Teerikangas & Very, 2006, p. 36). In a secondary process, adults experience organizational culture and have the chance to modify it in course of time while the primary organizational process continues to exist and influences the individuals (Teerikangas & Very, 2006, p. 37). Drumm (1991) specifically argues that organizational culture is a pattern of value judgment and assumptions of certain behavior which was introduced by individuals earlier and which has proven to be successful (Drumm, 1991, p. 61). Having those various definitions in mind one could summarize the term in stating that organizational culture is about a shared understanding among members of the organization (Weber & Camerer, 2003, p. 412).

Definition of Cultural Integration

But what exactly is cultural or human integration? Birkinshaw defines the human integration process from an organizational behavioral perspective and argues that satisfaction and the creation of a shared identity from employees are central (Birkinshaw et al., 2000, p. 398). The human integration process therefore aims at establishing a positive attitude from the employees towards the M&A integration process (Birkinshaw et al., 2000, p. 400) and the whole new organization respectively (Stahl & Voigt, 2008, p. 162). As a result, the company profits from the creation of a cultural community that is based on collective commitment (Bijlsma-Frankema, 2001, p. 198), because employees will have a positive standpoint with regards to the integration process. The question now rises how such a positive commitment can be reached. It is first of all essential to understand the employees involved in a M&A transaction and its behavior. Hill and Seo (2005) have established a conceptual framework including six theories in order to show how integration processes affect the psychological and behavioral responses (Seo & Hill, 2005, p. 425). Table 5 summarizes the theories and its main characteristics. The paper will then concentrate the key problems regarding the human integration process and outline factors that will help to overcome the problematic.

Human Integration Theories		
Theory	**Stress Factors**	**Outcome**
Anxiety Theory	Uncertainty, separation, anxiety	Low productivity, lack of motivation
Social Identity Theory	Loss of old identities	In-group-out-group phenomenon, refusal to change
Acculturation Theory	Adjustment to different organizational cultures	Stress, cultural clash, interorganizational conflicts or tensions
Role Conflict Theory	Ambiguous and conflicting roles	Low job satisfaction, low motivation
Job Characteristic Theory	Change of job characteristic and job environment	Job satisfaction and commitment versus absenteeism and low motivation
Organization Justice Theory	Perceived fairness of employees	Stress, turnover, lack of trust

Table 5 Theories with Regard to Human Integration in M&A Literature
Own elaboration according to Seo and Hill (2005), p.425

Merger Stress

A merger or acquisition process within a company always encompasses change. Often employees feel exposed to changes with respect to loss of power, insufficient information about the object behind the transaction, the struggle to survive, increasing work load and the influence on their privacy (Habeck, et al., 2002, p. 18). In fact, employees compare such as situation in the company with a loss of close family members or friends (Appelbaum, Gandell, Yortis, Proper, & Jobin, 2000, p. 654). As a natural consequence, employees of both, the acquiring and the acquired firm, face physical health problems (Marks, 1997, p. 268) as well as psychological pressure (Beth-von der Warth, 2004, p. 14). Feelings range from anxiety, anger and uncertainty over sorrow and resistance to the complete loss of trust. The worst outcome for the company is reached if the employee breaches its inner contract with the company (Beth-von der Warth, 2004, p. 14). From that point on, the employee will most likely switch into a negative and unproductive behavior. This phenomenon is known as the so called merger syndrome (Beth-von der Warth, 2004, p. 14; Colombo, Conca, Buongiorno, & Gnan, 2007, p. 204). During an integration process, employees show a defensive reaction as a result of stress and pressure which are expressed through different behavior patterns (Appelbaum, et al., 2000, p. 656). Such a behavior is communicated actively through voice or sabotage and/ or through passive reactions as for example absenteeism and shirking (Larsson & Finkelstein, 1999, p. 7).The burden of productivity loss (Bijlsma-Frankema, 2001, p. 193) and a cultural clash have to be carried by the company.

Us-versus-them

Another phenomenon that arises during the integration process is the us-versus-them view. This concept is a substantial part of the Social Identity Theory (Tajfel, 1981, p. 22; Turner, 1982, p. 16) and encompasses the in-and-out-group phenomenon. According to that theory, individuals are biased towards in-group members and value negatively the out group members (Stahl & Voigt, 2008, p. 162). To a certain extent, every company has to face this problematic; however this in-and-out group phenomenon is fostered in threatening business situations, especially in takeovers (Elsass & Veiga, 1994, p. 432; Hogg & Terry, 2000, p. 122). Particularly at the beginning of the pre-merger phase, the company has to bear the risk of loss of cooperation and motivation of the employees from both companies (Appelbaum et al., 2000, p. 654). The more structure, cultures and systems are integrated the higher is the possibility that this opportunistic behavior of the employees view will decrease (Appelbaum, et al., 2000, p. 654). However, if this mechanism is ignored by management, employees will experience negative feelings and avoid direct interaction with the new business entity (Bijlsma-Frankema, 2001, p. 194). This in turn increases the chance of a M&A failure.

Trust

One key factor that helps to overcome this scenario and fosters integration is trust (Bijlsma-Frankema, 2001, p. 199). Trust is defined as “the expectation that another’s action will be beneficial rather than detrimental” (Gambetta, 1988, p. 217). A firm that is involved in an integration process is challenged in building trust among two different organizational cultures. Trust creation asks for shared norms (Creed & Miles, 1996, p. 19) that helps to minimize risk of misinterpretation of mutual expectations (Bijlsma-Frankema, 2001, p. 200). But again, the question is how to achieve shared norms in an integration process that is accompanied by stress, pressure and uncertainty.

Communication

Communication could overcome this dilemma. Recent studies in M&A have proven that most of the employees are dissatisfied with the communication during an integration process (Buono & Bowditch, 2003, p. 196; Cartwright, 2005, p. 21). In fact, a study conducted by Inkypen, Sundaram & Rockwood (2000) clearly shows that European acquirer lack of effective communication as compared to the US firms (Inkpen, Sundaram, & Rockwood, 2000, p. 59). This fact should raise attention among the European firms as it is commonly known that communication clearly enhances employees' motivation (Appelbaum, 2000, p. 652). A study conducted by Nahass and colleagues (2008) clearly outlines the benefits of a fast communication: it increases, among others, employee's moral, the understanding of the company's direction, customer and quality focus, and the productivity (Nahass et al., 2008, p. 19). Communication during a transaction process requires special needs that differ from usual day-to-day communication in a firm. Therefore managers should invest on the on hand in communication that informs the employees about present and future activities and on the other hand in communication that enhances productivity (Buono & Bowditch, 2003, pp. 196-197). As communication aims at reducing uncertainty and trust among employees, management needs to communicate in an eloquent (Epstein, 2004, p. 177), clear and consistent way during the pre-merger phase (Appelbaum, et al., 2000, p. 658). Ranft (2002) proposes a face-to-face communication that enhances the mutual understanding and trust of the employees, fostering a more favorable atmosphere for cooperation and collaboration (Ranft & Lord, 2002, p. 437). Due to the fact that miscommunication results in negative feelings and polarization, there is an urgent need to communicate to all levels of employee considering various channels (Kavanagh & Askanasy, 2006, p. 97). Exemplary channels are newsletter and hotlines, presentations, realistic merger previews, workshops, counseling and survey feedback (Buono & Bowditch, 2003, pp. 201-210). As the provided analysis has shown, the human integration process is in fact a core element of the post-merger phase. The readiness of the employee is absolutely necessary (Epstein, 2004, p. 176) in order to continue with successfully integration structures and other tasks.

2.2.3 Task Integration

As mentioned in part 2.2, task integration consists of two main integration processes: Procedural integration and physical integration. The latter one encompasses product line integration and integration of production technologie, while procedural integration concentrates on legal and accounting integration, functional integration and SBU integration (Shrivastava, 1986, p. 68). According to Birkinshaw and colleagues (2000), task integration, based on the process perspective, describes the process of value creation which is assessed through capability transfer and resource sharing (Birkinshaw et al., 2000, p. 399). Value creation, in turn, can be seen as a long-term process (Stahl & Voigt, 2008, p. 164) that asks for the identification and realization of synergies (Birkinshaw et al., 2000, p. 400). In order to capture the whole picture of task integration and the resulting M&A performance, it is necessary to elaborate on the definition given by Birkinshaw and colleagues. For the purpose of the paper, it is of relevance to outline the two most important key concepts of task integration that is capability transfer and realization of synergies.

Capability Transfer

As mentioned above, task integration can be seen as value creation which encompasses the transfer of capability (Birkinshaw et al., 2000, p. 399). One central type of capability transfer consists of resource sharing, wherein the operating assets of the merging companies are combined and rationalized (Haspeslagh & Jemison, 1991, p. 29). Consequently, economies of scope as well as economies of scale are realized (Haspeslagh & Jemison, 1991, p. 29). From the organizational learning perspective, the transfer of capabilities leads to knowledge sharing and drives innovation as well as learning processes (Vermeulen & Barkema, 2001, p. 469). One major capability of a firm is knowledge, as it leads to value creation within the company (Haspeslagh & Jemison, 1991). Consequently, knowledge transfer can be seen as a substantial contributor to task integration. The concept of knowledge transfer has gained increased attention within the M&A research (Colombo, Conca, Buongiorno, & Gnan, 2007, p. 205; Darr & Kurtzberg, 2000, pp. 28-48; Ranft & Lord, 2002, pp. 420-440). Additional important capabilities are the functional skills and general entrepreneurial skills which strengthen the competitive advantage of the firm

(Haspeslagh & Jemison, 1991, pp. 30-31). The latter capability arises from the ability of the management to set corporate directions and make use of leadership skills (Haspeslagh & Jemison, 1991, p. 31). Functional skills are highly connected with knowledge and describe the ability to apply know-how in specific functional areas of the firm. As this skill often relates to the routine tasks, it seems difficult to transfer such skills within an M&A transaction (Haspeslagh & Jemison, 1991, p. 30). All of the capabilities of a firm are of importance. Haspeslagh and Jemison (1991), however, argue that the decisive capability of a firm consists in the creation of a unique combination of capabilities that leads to a competitive advantage (Haspeslagh & Jemison, 1991, p. 31) which in turn can be increased through the creation of new and complementary capabilities (Haspeslagh & Jemison, 1991, p. 32). At this point is seems obvious which strategic tool helps to realize this objective: A M&A transaction.

Synergy Realization

Referring to the definition given by Campell and Goold (1998), "the word synergy is derived from the word *synergos* which means 'working together.'" (Campbell & Goold, 1998, p. 139) In terms of business activities, a synergy effect is realized if the transferred capabilities of two firms strengthen the market position and consequently the returns of the companies (Haspeslagh & Jemison, 1991, p. 23). If the company manages to achieve positive synergies through changes, value is created. In contrast, negative synergies resulting from mismanagement may lead to value destruction (Schweiger & Very, 2003, p. 22). According to Schweiger and Very (2003), positive synergies can be achieved through cost synergies, revenue synergies, market power synergies and intangible synergies (Schweiger & Very, 2003, pp. 2-6). Table 7 gives a short overview of the named positive synergies:

Sources of Synergy Realization	
Types of Synergy	**Characteristic**
Cost Synergies	• Fixed cost reduction: Economies of scope and scale • Variables cost reduction: Increased purchasing power and productivity
Revenue Synergies	• Cross selling products or services through complementary sales organization or channels of distribution • Widening range of services and products
Market Power Synergies	• Elimination of competitors and capacity from the market • Increase of prices, margins and cash flows
Intangible Synergies	• Brand name extension; knowledge and know-how sharing • Intangible capability transfer

Table 6 Sources of Synergy Realization

Own illustration adopted from Schweiger and Very (2003), pp.4-6

The given insight into the concept of task integration shows a range of opportunities that arise with this type of integration. However, as the various tasks need to be integrated in multiple areas such as production, marketing, accounting and finance, problems may arise with respect to coordination, control and conflict resolution (Shrivastava, 1986, p. 66).

2.2.4 Speed of Integration

In practice, speed is likely to be perceived in a positive way. Most of the managers connect speed with process (Angwin, 2004, p. 418), development and success (Nahass et al., 2008, p. 2). It is widely assumed that fast integration serves as a tool to influence the development of coordination benefits and disruption costs within a M&A transaction (Puranam et al. 2009, p. 183). It is surprising, therefore, that up until now the concept of speed of integration did not enjoy sufficient attention in M&A literature. Only few researchers have tried to define the concept and aimed at finding a relationship between M&A performance and speed, as it can be seen within the following analysis. Speed of integration defines the time frame between deal closing and the finalization of the post merger integration phase. The time frame is defined by the degree of integration desired by the company (Homburg & Bucerius, 2006, p. 354). According to Angwin (2004), the importance of speed has increased within the M&A research as it promises long-term success and a competitive advantage for the company (Angwin, 2004, p. 418). The crucial question that arises when dealing with speed of integration in M&A transactions is whether a fast integration leads to an overall M&A success or a rather slow integration promises a positive M&A performance. Across M&A literature, M&A specialists debate this dilemma:

Angwin (2004) supports the idea that the first 100 days after integration determine integration success or failure, as early actions have larger effects on performance than later actions (Angwin, 2004, p. 428). Within this time frame, individuals of the companies expect change (Buono & Bowditch, 2003, p. 15) and managers could easily make use of these expectations. Angwin (2004) detects a relationship between the volume of changes made in the first 100 days and positive M&A performance in the third and fourth year (Angwin, 2004, p. 428). Ranft and Lord (2002) found in their study a positive relationship between speed and M&A performance. According to their findings, a fast integration leads to a more effective use of resources (Ranft & Lord, 2002, p. 438) which in turn leads to a competitive advantage on the market. Along with this argument of resource effectiveness, Beth-von der Warth outlines the positive effect of a fast synergy realization (Beth-von der Warth, 2004, p. 13). From a financial perspective, it appears that a high speed of integration generates a faster return on investment (Morag & Barakonyi, 2009, p. 57). In the field of behavioral theory, speed reduces uncertainty among employees (Angwin, 2004, p. 419; Homburg & Bucerius, 2006, p. 350) and potential power struggles (Beth-von der Warth, 2004, p. 12). A quick reaction in the beginning of the integration phase allows using the early enthusiasm of the stakeholders (Angwin, 2004, p. 420) and takes advantage of this positive atmosphere. Supporter of the organizational change perspective propose that a fast integration encourages stability of organizations involved (Angwin, 2004, p. 420; Morag & Barakonyi, 2009, p. 57). It is further argued that the events are more controllable with a fast integration (Angwin, 2004, p. 420). Additionally, with an increased speed, the merging firm can better face external threats, such as macro-economic, political (Angwin, 2004, p. 420) or legal barriers. A fast integration gives the chance to limit the time of reaction of the competitors (Angwin, 2004, p. 20). The arguments of a fast integration are supported by a study conducted by Nahass and colleagues (2008) among senior management of US companies who conducted a M&A transaction. The main outcome showed that the profitability was significantly higher when post-merger integration was conducted faster than normal. This effect was increased when the M&A process was completed in the first 100 days (Nahass et al., 2008, p. 15). Figure 6 visualizes this effect in comparing the deal performance of delayed and early integration.

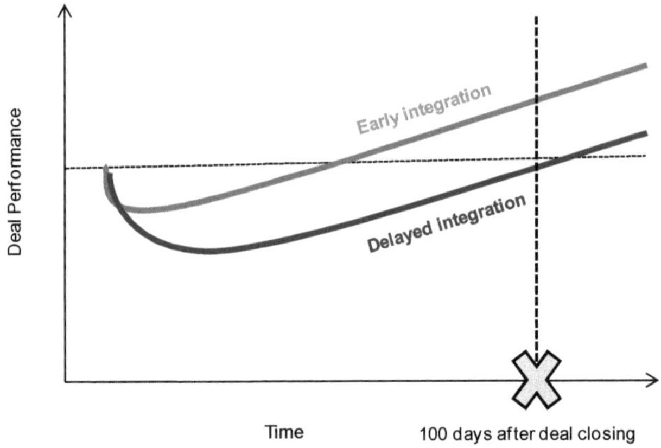

Figure 6 Deal Performance During Post-Merger Integration
Own elaboration according to Nahass et al (2005), p. 7

In contrast to this stream of literature, there are many researchers who favor slow integration. Relying on a study conducted by Olie (1994), slow integration reduces conflicts among employees (Olie, 1994, pp. 381-383). Further arguments are raised by Beth-von der Werth (2004) who argues that slow change encourages effective know-how transfer, high participation, careful planning, high motivation and a fluent transition to the new organization and its culture (Beth-von der Warth, 2004, p. 13).Those arguments for a slow integration are extended by Homburg and Bucerius (2006) who see fast integration as tool to foster turbulence and conflicts (Homburg & Bucerius, 2006, p. 351). A slow change allows for a longer time period for mutual understanding, trust building and the willingness to learn from each other (Buono & Bowditch, 2003, p. 15; Homburg & Bucerius, 2006, p. 351). DeMeuse (1987) compares the post-merger integration with a surgery of the company and promotes a slow integration: "Just as a patient needs to recover from a major surgery, an organization needs time to regain its strength. It takes time for people to understand their new roles, their new positions, to understand the new linkages, and get productive again." (DeMeuse, 1987, p. 1) Other studies found that there exists no relationship between speed an M&A performance at all (Bauer & Matzler, 2011, 2013)

To conclude, there is no right speed of integration, as it depends on other influencing variables (Bauer, 2012, p. 133) such as external relatedness, a firm's strategy, or the relative size of the companies (Bragado & Fuster, 1992, p. 27; Homburg & Bucerius, 2006, p. 347). No matter if a firm considers fast or slow integration it is essential to know that they are mutually exclusive (Beth-von der Warth, 2004, p. 12). But what is clear is that managers have to face the dilemma of integrating carefully or integrating fast (Bauer & Matzler, 2012, p. 6)

2.3 Problem Statement

As we can see in the previous section, speed is a decisive factor and somehow influences the overall M&A performance. The following literature review summarizes the most important studies that have been conducted in course of M&A research. The subsequent section will analyze the challenges that arise when dealing with speed of integration within the complex world of M&A transactions. Combining challenges and literature review, I will outline the research gap within the last part of this section.

2.3.1 Literature Review

The following intense literature review concentrates on three fields of research and its recent advances: The influence of human integration on M&A performance, the influence of task integration on M&A performance and finally the interrelation of speed of integration and M&A performance. Tables 7 to 9 summarize the empirical and conceptual papers of scientific and practice-oriented literature with regard to those topics.

Author	Sample	Method	Key Findings
Schweiger & Weber (1989)	Survey 178 HR-Managers	**Measuring** single phases of the merger	Systems and HR organization of the acquired company are integrated into acquiring company
Datta (1991)	Survey of 173 managers	**Independent variable**: organizational fit; relative size, integration process (marketing, function and production integration); **Dependent variable**: M&A performance	Compensation systems have no influence on M&A performance; Relative size has no influence on M&A performance; Different management systems show negative effect on M&A performance
Weber (1996)	Survey of 125 managers of 73 companies	**Independent variables:** organizational culture, removal of autonomy and commitment **Dependent variable**: change of ROA	High variance performance due to organizational culture and commitment and autonomy of the manager
Piske (2002)	Survey of 521 polish employees acquired by German firms	**Interdependent variable:** degree of integration, leadership characteristics **Dependent variable:** M&A performance	Positive relationship between degree of integration and M&A success; Management support only partly effects M&A success
Liao (2004)	Survey on 392 employees, 2 waves, horizontal transactions	**Measuring** the effect of organizational culture on the work characteristics of the employees and their commitment	Different work characteristics of employees decrease with increasing duration of integration; In course of integration, differences in evaluation of M&A success with respect to employees of buyer and target company
Schweiger & Goulet (2005)	Survey of employees of 120 target firm and 116 acquiring firm	**Variables:** Understanding of the culture, cultural difference, communication, trust, commitment, cooperation, cultural acceptance	Interventions on cultural learning of employees have a positive impact and lead to constructive behavior of the employees; Those interventions accelerate synergy realization and M&A performance
Kavanagh & Ashkanasy (2006)	Qualitative (63 experts opinion) and quantitative (454 employees of public organizations) research, 3	**Measurement** of cultural change, subdividing culture in power, role, task and person. Collecting	Choice of integration system is decisive for M&A outcome; The higher cultural change the more resistance show employees

	waves	More characteristics through qualitative interviews.	
Kolesky (2004)	Survey of 48 companies	**Independent variable:** support of communication and interaction, learning process, acceptance, changing processes **Depended variable**: process of integration	Support of communication and acceptance of change positively influences the integration process; Learning process and support of interaction has no significant influence on integration process
Slangen (2006)	Analysis of 106 transactions conducted by 96 companies	**Independent variable**: cultural distance, degree of integration **Dependent variable:** M&A performance	Similarity positively influences M&A performance; High degree of integration negatively influence M&A performance if cultural distance is high
Teerinkangas & Very (2006)	Analysis of 19 empirical studies	**Independent variables:** inter alia management style, reward and evaluation systems, risk taking, lateral integration	Culture as a decisive factor for integration; Integration influences the culture-performance-relationship; Lack of adequate measurement model "culture"
Stahl & Voigt (2008)	Meta-analysis of 46 studies	**Independent Variable:** cultural differences, socio-cultural integration **Controls:** degree of relatedness **Dependent variable**: synergy realization, shareholder value	Cultural differences negatively impact integration; Cultural differences have no impact on synergy realization

Table 7 Relationship Human Integration and M&A Performance
Own elaboration according to M&A literature (see bibliography)

Author	Sample	Method	Key Findings
Larsson & Finkelstein (1999)	Case survey method: 112 transactions	**Independent variable:** complementarity, degree of integration **Dependent variable**: synergy realization	Complementarity is a decisive factor for synergy realization; Additional leverage effect through degree of integration
Zollo & Singh (2004)	Analysis of 228 transactions	**Independent variable:** codification of knowledge, acquisition experience, degree of integration **Control variable:** degree of relatedness, resource quality; **Dependent variable**: performance	Degree of integration has a significantly positive effect on M&A performance; Codification of knowledge has a positive effect on M&A performance; Acquisition experience: No significant influence on M&A performance;
Puranam, Singh & Zollo (2006)	Analysis of 207 transactions of 49 buyer companies	**Independent variable**: structural integration; **Control variable:** inter alia target size, average personnel cost; **Dependent variable:** performance of innovation	Structural integration influences innovation performance positively after a certain period of time
Puranam & Srikanth (2007)	Analysis of 97 transactions conducted by 43 buyer companies	**Independent variable:** structural integration, degree of technological similarity, target size and age, etc. **Dependent variable:** usage of innovation resources and knowledge	Positive relationship between structural integration and knowledge usage; Negative Relationship between structural integration and usage of innovation resources
Puranam, Singh & Chaudhuri (2009)	Analysis of 209 transaction conducted by 49 buyer companies	**Investigated variables:** structural integration, Technology, Common ground (comm. knowledge about technologies)	Common ground leads to a low demand of structural integration → integration through informal communication

		Control variable: target size and age, etc.	
Bresman, Birkinshaw &Nobel (2010)	Questionnaire (110 managers of 15 companies) and 3 case studies, R&D industry	**Independent variable:** Communication, visits and meetings, articulability of knowledge, time elapsed, size of unit **Dependent variable**: knowledge transfer: acquiring to acquired; acquired to acquiring	Communication and visits and meeting are significant predictors of technological know-how transfer. Time and articularibility depend on kind of knowledge; Immediate post-acquisition period is characterized by imposed knowledge transfer one way, but over time reciprocal knowledge transfer

Table 8 Relationship Task Integration and M&A Performance
Own elaboration according to existing M&A literature (see bibliography)

Author	Sample	Method	Key Findings
Positive Performance Effects			
Birkinshaw, Bresman & Hakanson (2000)	Case study on 3 companies, 2 waves of data collection	**Independent variable:** task integration, human integration **Dependent variable:** M&A success	Speed as a decisive factor for M&A performance; Human and task integration occur at different speeds; Renewed task integration is built on the success of achieved human integration
Inkpen, Sundaram, Rockwood (2000)	Six case studies of Silicon-Valley-type companies acquired by non-U.S firms (all from the EU)	**Investigated Variables:** deal value, average size, extent of information leakage, etc.	Geographic proximity influences the speed of integration; the smaller the distance the faster integration European companies show slower response time then US companies – hinders product development and market opportunities
Gates & Very (2003)	Survey of 53 managers	**Investigated variables:** acquirers strategy, sources of value creation and value leakage, integration plan	Integration in first 100 days creates atmosphere for successful synergy exploitation and therefore leads to M&A success; Outcome of the integration are to be obtained at the set milestone
Schlützen & Jöns (2003)	20 experts interviews	Standardized interviews regarding success factors of transaction	Speed of integration as a decisive factor; “Window of opportunity” as defined and limited time frame for integration , crucial for uncertainty avoidance and trust building;

			Speed of integration depends on variables such as resources, integration management, etc.
Angwin (2004)	Survey with 232 corporate acquisitions	**Independent Variable:** changes **Dependent variable:** inter alia performance, degree of integration, usage of synergy, cultural integration, etc.	Fast integration is beneficial: less uncertainty among employees, faster return on investment fast integration shows beneficial effect in long term performance, after 3 yrs.
Homburg & Bucerius (2005)	232 managers from acquiring firms	**Independent Variable:** degree of integration; speed of integration; cost reduction; market related performance; **Dependent variable:** financial performance;	Positive and significant relationship of speed of integration and market-related performance after the acquisition; Limits costumer uncertainty
Homburg & Bucerius (2006)	Survey with 232 horizontal M&A's	**Independent variable:** speed of integration **Controls:** similarities in target markets, market position, strategic orientation, management style **Dependent variable:** M&A success ; relatedness	Speed of integration is positively related to integration and market performance; High speed favorable if high internal similarities; Companies with high relatedness can realize high speed
Colombo, Conca, Buogiorno & Gnan (2007)	Survey of 67 managers responsible for international transactions	**Independent variable:** planning, acquisition experience, knowledge, new usage of management resources, organizational climate, start of integration after closing **Dependent variable:** performance	A delayed start of integration negatively influence the M&A performance
Cording, Christman & King (2008)	Survey with 129 horizontal transactions	**Independent Variable:** speed and depth of integration; fluctuation of top management; market and customer focus **Controls**: acquisition experi-	Positive effect on external reorganization and consequently direct Positive effect of speed of integration on market-expansion

		ence, relative size, ROE, etc. **Dependent variable**: performance, Market Expansion, internal reorganization	
Schlaepfer et al. (2008)	Survey of 55 companies	Descriptive study	Speed of integration is a M&A success factor Majority of companies finalize integration after 12 months
Negative performance effects			
Ranft & Lord (2002)	7 case studies	**Independent variables:** Nature of underlying knowledge, management practices, acquisition context, key dimensions of implementation **Dependent variable:** transfer of technologies and capabilities	Slow implementation allows for learning effect → "window of opportunity"; Dilemma of preserving knowledge of acquired firm and the need to integrate knowledge; Open communication facilitates transfer
Nahavadi & Malekzadeh (1988)	Collection of literature	**Analysis of influencing variables:** modes of acculturation, acculturative stress, Characteristics of target and buyer company Dependent variable: Successful implementation of the merger	Slow integration promotes positively the M&A transaction; Understanding and reconciliation of differences need time
Bijlsma Frankema (2001)	Qualitative study, Analysis of 42 case studies	**Analysis of variables** such as culture, role of management, tasks and capacities, psychological safety, etc.	Trust building demands time; Slow integration is beneficial; High speed would have detrimental consequences for value creation
Olie (1994)	Multiple case study	**Analysis of variables** such as degree of compatibility of administrative practices, management style, organizational structure	Minimization of conflicts between employees of merging firms
No significant performance effects			
Wille, Bauer & Anslinger (2011)	72 transactions	**Independent variables:** brand and performance program fit,	Slow integration important for sustainable resources; Significant effect of speed on M&A performance not proven

		degree of integration, speed of integration, resource reduction **Controls:** relative size, target markets, type of transaction, brand integration strategy; **Dependent variable:** performance	
Bauer & Matzler (2013)	Survey with 106 companies	**Independent Variable**: strategic similarity, cultural compatibility, degree of integration, speed of integration **Controls**: type of transaction, relative size, industry growth, institutional distance **Dependent Variable:** M&A success	No significant relationship between speed of integration and M&A performance

Table 9 Relationship Speed of Integration and M&A Performance
Own elaboration according to various literatures (see bibliography)

As the literature review shows, there have been several studies regarding human integration, task integration and speed of integration. Especially the existing literature on human integration shows the increasing awareness of the human factor in a M&A transaction. Despite the research advances in all three research areas, there remains a high failure rate in M&A transactions (Cartwright & Schoenberg, 2006, p. 4). Consequently, there is obviously a need to improve M&A research. Research gaps exist in literature regarding human integration (Datta, 1991, p. 281; Nahavandi & Malekzadeh, 1988, p. 79; Teerikangas & Very, 2006, p. 31) and task integration (Schweiger & Very, 2003, p. 1). The most significant work that needs to be done, however, is on speed of integration. The following paragraph outlines the challenges that have not been solved by recent literature so far.

2.3.2 Challenges of M&A Integration and Speed

As the M&A research with respect to speed of integration is still in its infancy, there are several challenges or research gaps respectively. The challenges analyzed in this chapter rely on the findings of Bauer and Anslinger (2012) who outline three fields of problems regarding speed of integration: Speed-performance-relationship, deterministic factors and measurements of speed of integration (Bauer & Anslinger, 2012, p. 211).

Speed-Performance-Relationship

As outlined in section 2.2.4, there are no clear results of whether speed of integration has a positive, negative or no effect at all on the M&A performance. It is disputable whether one can categorize the speed of integration in simply “fast or slow” (Bauer & Anslinger, 2012, p. 213), which consequently leads more or less to a trap of black and white thinking. The question arises whether managers can freely choose among the ranges of speed of integration or if there are certain factors that might influence and limit the decision making process. In order to capture and understand the speed-performance-relationship ,Bauer and Anslinger (2012) propose to empirically analyze the value creating mechanisms and to expand the group respondents including CEOs and employees. (Bauer & Anslinger, 2012, p. 18).

Deterministic Factors

According to Bauer and Anslinger (2012), three factors influence and limit the choice of speed of integration: Systematic conditions, Pre-merger factors and post-merger factors (Bauer & Anslinger, 2012, pp. 213-216). Homburg and Bucerius (2004), for example, developed several criteria in order to decide on the right path of integration. They argue that speed of integration depends on internal and external relatedness of the firms (Homburg & Bucerius, 2006, pp. 350-353). A detailed overview of addtional factors can be taken from the Figure 7. This table provides a snapshot of influencing factors and it becomes clear that there are definitely more factors that would lead to more exact and reliable implications for M&A management (Bauer & Anslinger, 2012, p. 218).

Speed of Integration Measurement

An additional explanation of the different results of the M&A research with respect to speed of integration and M&A performance could be the inefficient usage of the measurement of speed of integration (Bauer & Anslinger, 2012, p. 215). Previous studies have measured the speed of integration in terms of a single measurement item (Cording, Christman, & King, 2008, p. 761; Schlaepfer et al., 2008; Wille, Bauer, & Anslinger, 2011, p. 163). As shown in section 2.2., the M&A integration is a complex field in which the different organizational levels are integrated. It is therefore questionable if all of the organizational levels require the same speed of integration (Birkinshaw et al., 2000, pp. 365-400.; Olie, 1994, p. 383.; Ranft & Lord, 2002, p. 423). The integration of production or supply sources are, for example, much faster achieved than an integration of a complex organizational culture. This underlies the argument of Bauer & Anslinger (2012) who regard a single item measurement as insufficient in order to capture the whole construct of speed (Bauer & Anslinger, 2012, p. 219). Figure 7 summarizes the complexity of challenges that arises within the concept of speed of integration. In the course of the paper, focus is given on the speed-performance-relationship and the assessment of speed.

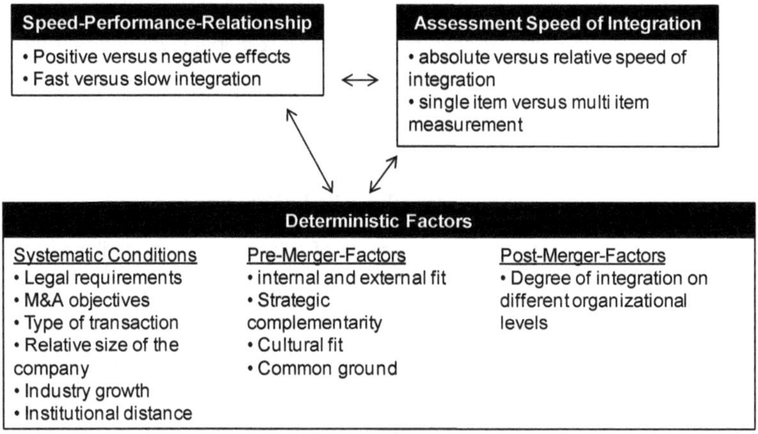

Figure 7 Challenges Speed of Integration
Own elaboration according to Bauer & Anslinger (2012), p. 213-219

2.3.3 Research Gap

The empirical overview leaves us with an unsatisfying answer. There is a lack of evidence, whether speed of integration has a positive, negative or no effect at all on the overall M&A performance. After years of research, managers still face the dilemma of integrating as fast as possible or of integrating rather slow and careful. Thus it seems to be obvious that there is much more research to be done, relying on the statement of Homburg and Bucerius (2006) who argue that "prior research on post-merger integration (PMI) has largely neglected the issue of speed at which integration should take place" (Homburg & Bucerius, 2006, p. 347) . To solve the research gap, Bauer and Anslinger (2012) propose a complex and integrative model. At the same time they argue that such as model would not applicable in practice as the speed of integration in all its facets and interactions with other variables would go beyond a useful model. Therefore, it is more advisable to focus on detailed aspects (Bauer & Anslinger, 2012, p. 219)

One decisive aspect that has to be detected is the question of how exactly the integration speed of the different organizational levels influence the overall M&A performance. As stated in section 2.3.2 , it is questionable if all of the organizational levels require the same speed of integration (Birkinshaw,

Bresman, & Hakanson, 2000, pp. 399-400; Olie, 1994, p. 383.; Ranft & Lord, 2002, p. 423). It might be the case that one organizational level needs a much longer time for integration than the other organizational level. Furthermore, one could argue that the different organizational levels depend on each other. In proving those statements, the paper will shed light into the area of integration speed and explain the contradicting findings that have been made so far.

The study aims at providing concepts of solutions for the challenges that have been raised during the few years of speed of integration research. Within this work, I will give a closer look into the speed of integration and M&A performance while focusing on the deterministic factors in the post-merger phase. In doing so, I rely on the theoretical implications of Bauer and Matzler (2012) suggesting that future research may test existing hypotheses with the new measurement model (Bauer & Matzler, 2012, p. 17).

3 Research Model and Hypotheses Development

The previous chapter clearly outlined the difficulties with respect to speed of integration and the M&A performance. The present chapter provides a value adding research model that contributes to filling the gaps of research within the field of speed of integration. Based on this model, three hypotheses are developed.

3.1 Research Model

As stated in section 2.2.2 and 2.2.3, two main organizational levels within the integration process are the human integration and task integration. In order to discover the interrelation of both with M&A performance, the paper develops a model built on the findings of Birkinshaw and colleagues (Birkinshaw et al., 2000, p. 421).

Underlying model

At this point, the main argumentation underlying the model of Birkinshaw and colleagues are explained first before the actual research model of the paper is developed. The model of Birkinshaw and colleagues assumes a clear distinction between human and task integration as the latter one is based on the process school while the former one is built on behavioral school (Birkinshaw et al., 2000, p. 399). Additionally, they vary in their managerial approaches and its objectives (Birkinshaw et al., 2000, p. 400). In a paradoxical manner, both organizational levels are to a certain degree interdependent while at the same time they diverge. Consequently, human integration might be integrated faster than task integration and vice versa. Birkinshaw and colleagues reason that "a relative emphasis on either task or human integration can potentially have a significant negative impact on the outcome of the acquisition." (Birkinshaw et al., 2000, p. 399) A decisive factor that may help to overcome this dilemma and that may increase the effectiveness of both, human and task integration, is speed. Birkinshaw and colleagues suggest that the two organizational levels may occur at different levels of speeds (Birkinshaw et al., 2000, p. 399). To summarize the arguments: Birkinshaw and colleagues assume that the M&A performance is a function of human and task integration which are parallel processes. The study provides various interesting outcomes. The decisive finding for the present study, however, states that "the human integration process appears to facilitate the effectiveness of task integration process" (Birkinshaw et al., 2000, p. 419). Consequently, the human integration functions as a basis of task integration and hence the M&A performance. The study indicates that firms show problems if task integration occurred faster than human integration, as the individuals were affected by uncertainty with respect to their new colleagues and management (Birkinshaw et al., 2000, p. 419). The overall findings are graphically illustrated and summarized in Figure 8:

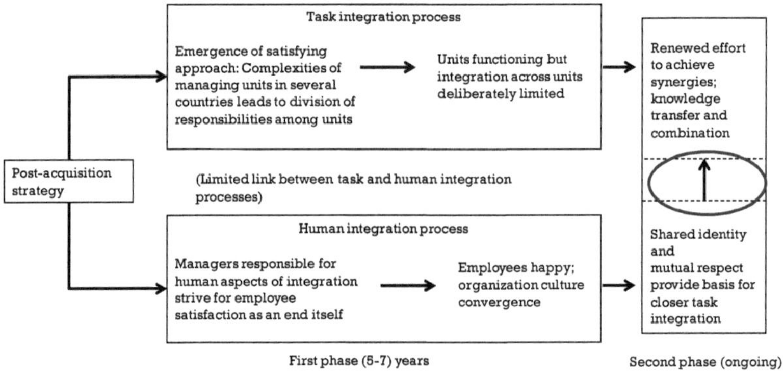

Figure 8 Influence of Task and Human Integration on M&A Performance
Own elaboration according to Birkinshaw et. al (2000), p. 421

Research Model

The present research model elaborates on the findings of Birkinshaw and colleagues in concentrating on the issue of speed of integration. It determines the effects of speed of task integration on M&A performance and the role of human integration within this relationship. It is the aim to identify how the speed of human integration leverages the effect of task integration speed and M&A performance. Additionally, the model serves as a tool to investigate the favorable pace that firms choose for an effective integration. Drawn together, the aforementioned arguments suggest a framework consisting of the independent variables task integration speed and human integration speed, as well as the dependent variable M&A performance. Figure 9 presents the research model at hand:

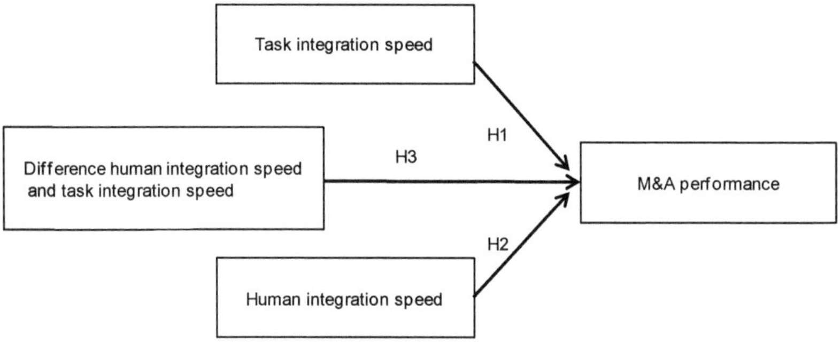

Figure 9 Research Model
Own elaboration

3.2 Hypotheses Development

Having established the research model, the following part develops all three hypotheses by analyzing the influential effects of task integration speed and human integration speed on the M&A performance. The hypotheses development continues by illustrating the influence on the difference of human integration speed and task integration speed on overall M&A performance respectively. Recapturing the concept of task and human integration presented in part 2.2 and the approaches presented in the model of Birkinshaw and colleagues, it is now possible to form an overall picture of task and human integration and consequently to create the three hypotheses. As Birkinshaw and colleagues (2000) recommend, both integration processes are regarded as a separate processes (Birkinshaw et al., 2000, p.399). This argument is supported by Bauer and Matzler (2012) who argue that the separation of task and human integration in terms of speed is very beneficial (Bauer & Matzler, 2012, p. 17). There have been various studies about the impacts of speed of integration on M&A performance which can be seen in the literature review section 2.3.1. However, up to best my knowledge, only one study conducted by Bauer, Degischer and Matzler (2013) separated the speed of integration in task and human integration when analyzing its impact on M&A performance (Bauer, Degischer, & Matzler, 2013, p. 2). The present study expands on this field and separates both operational types of integration.

As outlined in section 2.2.4, there is a range of arguments that favor fast task integration as it provides for example a rapid transfer of capabilities, an earlier implementation and more effective usage of resources and a fast synergy realization (Angwin, 2004, p. 428; Beth-von der Warth, 2004, p. 13, Homburg & Bucerius, 2006, p. 350). Despite those reasonable arguments, I rely on the conclusion brought forward by Birkinshaw and colleagues, who reason that mutual respect and trust form a basis for capability transfer and consequently synergy realization (Birkinshaw et al., 2000, p. 419). Another reasonable argument for a slow integration derives from the fact that it creates time necessary to introduce and distribute responsibilities (Birkinshaw et al., 2000, p. 419) and know-how (Beth-von der Warth, 2004, p. 13) to the employees of the acquiring and acquired company. Consequently, it reduces the risk of negative synergy creation which in turn would lead to value destruction (Schweiger & Very, 2003, p. 4). As task integration has to be realized in various areas such as production, marketing, accounting and finance, each of the fields are potential sources for loss of control, coordination problems and conflicts (Shrivastava, 1986, p. 66). Built on the facts outlined above, the resulting hypothesis can be summarized as follows:

Hypothesis 1: The speed of task integration process negatively influences the M&A performance.

Organizational culture is seen as the key factor for M&A performance (Schweiger & Goulet, 2005).The human integration is therefore a decisive factor as it provides satisfaction and a shared identity for the employees (Birkinshaw, et al., 2000, p. 398). Referring to the PricewaterhouseCoopers 11th Annual CEO survey, 60% of US respondents see cultural issues and conflicts as the greatest obstacle to M&A success (Nahass, et al., 2008, p. 28). As outlined in section 2.2.2, the complex field of human integration is connected with various problems such as merger syndrome (Beth-von der Warth, 2004, p. 14) in connection with defensive and passive reactions of the employees (Larsson & Finkelstein, 1999, p. 7). The human integration is therefore an essential part to enhance M&A performance. As humans represent the most important resource of the company, it is of importance to enhance their commitment and loyalty during a M&A transaction. The faster those goals are reached; the better will be the outcome of the overall M&A process, due to the fact that speed positively influences the employee's behavior (Angwin, 2004, p.419). As already outline in section 2.2.2, a fast integration is beneficial for individuals as it leads, among others, to a reduction of uncertainty (Angwin D. , 2004, p. 419; Homburg & Bucerius, 2006, p. 350) and power struggle (Beth-von der Warth, 2004, p. 12), stabilization of organization (Angwin D. , 2004, p. 420; Morag & Barakonyi, 2009, p. 57) and profit from early enthusiasm (Buono & Bowditch, 2003, p. 15). Based on the positive factors of human integration and its effect within the company, the second hypothesis reads as follows:

Hypothesis 2: The speed of the human integration process positively influences the overall M&A outcome.

Having in mind the argumentation presented above, it is now intuitively logical to assume that human integration has to be realized before task integration is completed. Supporting this argument Gates and Very (2003) claim that "once an appropriate atmosphere has been created; the acquirer can focus on the 'capability transfer' stage." (Gates & Very, 2003, p. 170). I argue that human integration speed functions as a leverage effect as it will strengthen the influence of task integration speed on M&A performance. If the buyer company reduces the uncertainty and gains commitment among the employees, they will work together, profit from each other, transfer knowledge and other capabilities, which leads to a realization of synergies and value creation (Haspeslagh & Jemison, 1991, p. 23). Indications of such an effect have also been made available in the study conducted by Nahass and colleagues (2008): 31% of the respondents claimed a productivity growth if employee communication was realized fast. Furthermore, employees' moral and enthusiasm increased with a fast communication (Nahass, et al., 2008, p. 18). Based on those arguments, the following hypothesis forms the object of investigation:

Hypothesis 3: If human integration speed is faster than the task integration speed the effect on M&A performance is positive.

4 Methodology

Once the measurement model with its respective hypotheses is developed, the following part outlines the different measurement methods of each construct. Subsequently, the sample and its data is presented. Section four concludes with an analysis of the results and its evaluation respectively.

4.1 Measurement Development

Following the advice of King, Dalton, Daily and Covin (2004), the constructs are based on existing models and items (King, Dalton, Daily, & Covin, 2004, p. 188). The following part identifies the appropriate models that are used to explain the variables of the research model. It will concentrate on the independent variables, followed by the dependent variable, and finally the control variables.

Relative Speed of Integration

In order to develop a measurement for task integration speed and human integration speed it is necessary to define the concept of speed of integration. As defined in part 2.2.3, speed of integration represents the time frame from deal closing to the desired degree of integration (Homburg & Bucerius, 2006, p. 354). The speed of integration of both, the task and human integration process, is measured with a new model created by Bauer and Matzler (2012) which measures the relative speed of integration (Bauer & Matzler, 2012, p. 9). Figure 10 represents the respective formula:

$$Relative\ Speed\ = \frac{Degree\ of\ Change\ on\ organizational\ level}{Scalepoints\ of\ Duration\ of\ integration} * Duration\ of\ integration$$

Figure 10 Relative Speed of Integration
Bauer & Matzler (2012), p. 9

This model is used as it provides more statistical reliability and volatility. Furthermore it overcomes the problem of inconclusive results which have been experienced in past studies related to speed of integration (Bauer & Matzler, 2012, p. 17). For the purpose of the research question, a separation of task and human integration is considered in the following parts.

4.1.1 Independent Variable

The following chapter outlines the measurement models of the two independent variables, which are task integration speed and human integration speed.

Task integration speed

As already mentioned, one independent variable of the model is task integration speed. Relying on the measurement model of Cording et al. (2008), the degree of change is assessed on three organizational levels: integration of production (measured with two items), marketing integration (measured with three items) and system integration (measured with three items), which all can be summarized to task integration (Cording, Christman, & King, 2008, p. 761). The degree of change is determined on a seven point scale, ranging from 1 *(no change at all)* to 7 *(complete change)*. Figure 11 visualizes the measurement model of task integration

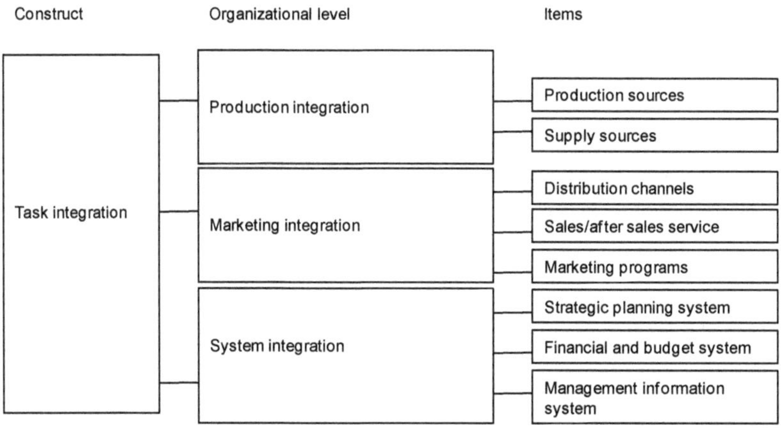

Figure 11 Operationalization Degree of Task Integration
Own elaboration according to Cording et al. (2008), p.761

In order to assess the relative speed completely, the duration of integration is needed. Here again, the paper relies on the same levels used for the degree of integration created by Cording (2008). Consequently, the duration of integration is operationalized with three items: integration of production, marketing integration and system integration (Cording et al., 2008, p. 761). The measurement ranges from 1 *(longer than 24 months)* to 7 *(less than six months)*. Having assessed the degree and duration of the various levels (see Figure 12), it is now possible to calculate the relative speed of the different levels of task integration which equals the degree of change on the respective organizational level, divided by the scale points of duration of each type of task integration times the duration of the types of task integration.

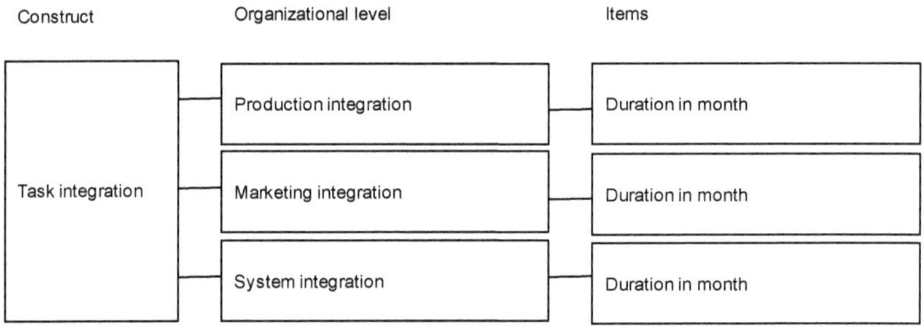

Figure 12 Operationalization Duration Task Integration
Own elaboration according to Cording et al. (2008), p. 761

Human Integration Speed

The independent variable of human integration speed is to be said to influence the M&A performance. Contradicting to the task integration speed, human integration speed affects the performance in a positive way. In other words: A fast integration of cultural and human aspects will foster M&A success. In order to develop a measurement model for the independent variable human integration speed, a similar approach compared to task integration speed is used. The formula of relative speed serves as a basis. The degree of change is measured with the level of socio- cultural integration which consists of three items (see Figure 13) (Cording et al., 2008, p. 761). Again, the degree of change is assessed on a 7-point scale ranging from ranging from 1 *(no change at all)* to 7 *(complete change)*.

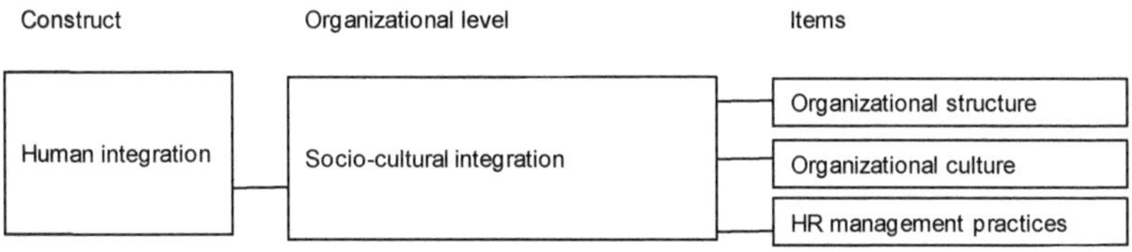

Figure 13 Operationalization Degree of Human Integration
Own elaboration according to Cording et al.(2008), p. 761

As presented in Figure 14, the duration of human integration consists of one item and is measured on a scale ranging from 1 *(longer than 24 months)* to 7 *(less than six months).* The relative speed of human integration can now be calculated by the degree of change on the socio-cultural integration, divided by the scale points of duration of socio-cultural integration times the duration of socio-cultural integration.

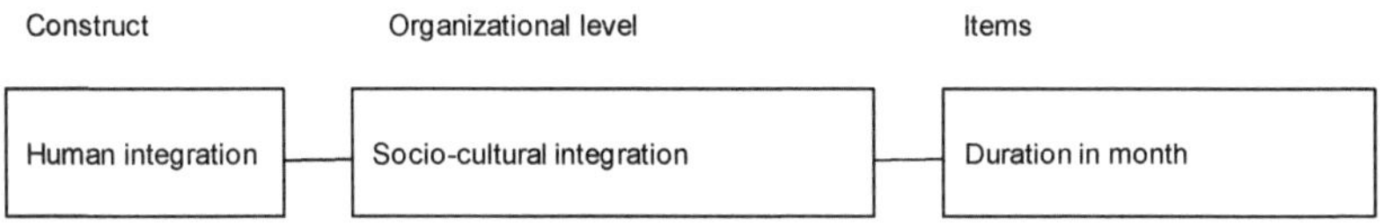

Figure 14 Operationalization Duration Human Integration
Own elaboration according to Cording et al. (2008), p. 761

4.1.2 Dependent Variable

In the present research model M&A performance serves as the dependent variable. In course of the M&A research, scientists tried to find an accurate measurement for the M&A performance. However there has been no agreement on a universal measurement model. Zollo and Meier (2008) address exactly this problem. Research approaches vary across different levels, from subjective to objective measurements, from short-term to long-term time period, from organizational level of analysis to a process level (Zollo & Meier, 2008, p. 55). Angwin (2004), for example, defined four dimensions with respect to M&A performance. The dimensions consist of overall performance (i.e. overall success; achievement of strategic goals), followed by financial performance (i.e. recovery of cost of capital; group profitability), integration (i.e. technological benefits; operational, cultural and IT integration) and market R&D (i.e. market share gain; increase in sales volume; product development) (Angwin , 2004, p. 424). According to Teerikangas & Very (2006) the M&A performance depends on cultural differences that are mediated by the integration strategy, the selected acculturative modes, the progress of cultural integration and the managerial efforts during the M&A phase (Teerikangas & Very, 2006, p. 38). The present research model however will rely on the proposed steps by Becker (2005), combing the objective success methods and subjective success methods (Becker, 2005, pp. 336-337). It measures each dimension with four indicators on a seven point scale ranging from 1 *(strong negative development/ absolutely not agree)* over 4 *(no development/neutral)* to 7 *(strong positive development/absolutely agree).* The respondents were asked to set the items in relation to the situation prior the transaction. Figure 15 represents the operationalization of the construct M&A performance:

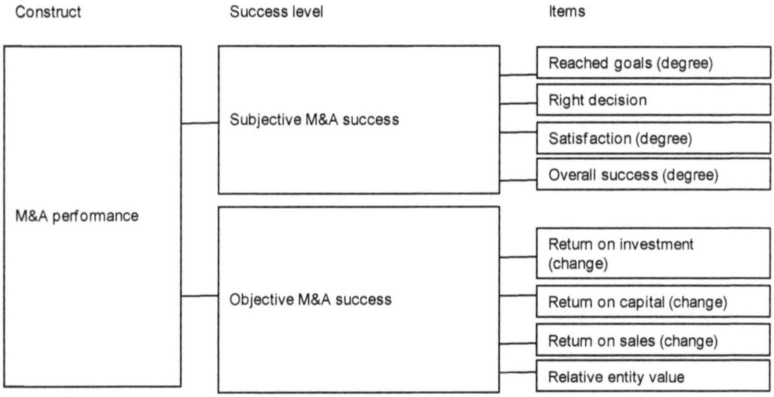

Figure 15 Operationalization M&A Performance
Own elaboration according to Becker (2005), p. 336-337

The objective M&A success defines the quantitative success factors, such as the return on equity, return on capital, return on sales and relative entity values. Whereas the subjective M&A success describes items like reached goals, right decision, satisfaction and overall success that all rely on estimation, preferences and valuation of individuals (Becker, 2005, pp. 336-346). As applied before, all of the items were collected with the help of closed questions.

4.1.3 Control Variables

A fourth category of the explained variables consists of control variables which are likely to, additionally to the independent variable, influence the M&A performance. For the purpose of this study the following control variables are tested:

- Relative size of the target company compared to the buyer company with respect to the turnover of the year previous to the transaction: <25%, 24%-49%; 50%-74%; 75%-100%; >100%
- Average industry growth during the last three years before the transaction: >-15%; -15% to -5%; -5%-0%; 0%-5%; 5%-10%; 11%-20%; 21%-30%; >30
- Actual annual turnover of the integrated company: <25 m €; 25-49 m €; 50-99 m €; 100-249 m €; 250-499 m €; 500-1000 m €; >1000 m
- Realized transactions during the last five years previous to the presented transaction: none; 1-2; 3-4; 5-6; >7

4.2 Sample and Data

The following part gives an overview about the sample and its collection. It concentrates on the methods used for the collection, the design of the questionnaire, followed by the pretest that was conducted beforehand, the data collection itself and finally the evaluation methods.

4.2.1 Sample

The M&A sample was identified on the basis of the Zephyr database of the Bureau van Dijk. The sample size includes companies, which are operating within the DACH regions that are Germany, Austria and Switzerland. As the study concentrates on mergers and acquisitions, only companies involved in those kind of transactions where asked. A further criterion is the transaction period. The study only includes companies who had their M&A deals completed between 2007 and 2010. This is an appropriate time frame as it is assumes that an evaluation on the M&A performance can be drawn at present. Table 10 captures the sample characteristics:

Sample Restrictions		
Criteria	**Characteristic**	**Sample**
Geographic area (buyer)	Germany, Switzerland and Austria	46,001
Time frame	January 01, 2007 – December 31, 2010	423,662
Type of transaction	Mergers and acquisitions	436,546
Major sectors	Primary sector, food, textile, wood, publishing, etc.	590,893
Current deal status	Completed	677,806

Table 10 Sample Restrictions
Own Elaboration according to the Zephyr Databank of Bureau van Dijk

Relying on the restrictions given in the table, we contacted 1,273 managers from 765 companies. However, only 561 can be taken into consideration as 204 firms were either insolvent or never involved in any transaction. It is further assumed, that some participants were not in the position to give a set of information referring to the whole M&A process as they have only participated in one particular process.

4.2.2 Data

In order to collect primary data, generally, a survey methodology is used wherein data is collected at one point in time. This survey can be conducted through different modes: mail, personal, email or internet and telephone. All of the four methods have their benefits and drawbacks (Ebster, 1999, p. 92-93; Hollensen, 2007, pp. 161-162). Based on the findings of Hollensen (2007), Table11 gives an overview of the different methods.

Survey Tools				
Questions	Postal mail	Internet/email	Telephone	Personal
Flexibility (ability to clarify problems)	✓	✓✓✓	✓✓✓	✓✓✓✓
Possibility of in-depth information	✓✓	✓	✓✓	✓✓✓✓
Use of visual aids	✓✓✓	✓✓✓✓	✓	✓✓✓
Possibility of widely dispersed sample	✓✓✓✓	✓✓✓✓	✓✓✓✓	✓✓
Response rates	✓	✓✓	✓✓✓	✓✓
Asking sensitive questions	✓✓✓	✓	✓	✓✓
Control of interviewer effect	✓✓✓✓	✓✓	✓✓	✓
Speed of data collection	✓	✓✓✓✓	✓✓✓✓	✓✓✓
Costs	✓✓✓	✓✓✓✓	✓✓✓✓	✓

Table 11 Survey Tools
Own elaboration according to Hollensen (2007), pp. 161-162

For the purpose of this survey, three cost moderate methods seemed adequate: mail, telephone and internet. This decision is based on the three criteria. First of all, only a relative restricted amount of resources in terms of money, time and personnel were available. A second aspect arises from the fact that the methods facilitated the contacting of the top level management, our key informants. Depending on their preferences, they were allowed to choose among the offered tools ranging from filling out the questionnaire on paper and send it back via post or email, using the online tool or participating on a telephone interview. The range of alternatives was highly appreciated by the top management. A third decision criterion is that the combination of the three methods captured a relative high amount of the limited universe of the sample and increased the response rate (Hollensen, 2007, p. 162).

Questionnaire Design

Based on the measurement development represented in part 4.1, a questionnaire was designed (see Appendix C). The questionnaire aims at interviewing top management. Here the key informant bias could be regarded as serious threat, but the managers of the acquiring firms seem to be the most knowledgeable persons involved in the M&A transaction (Datta, 1991, p. 282). Additionally, it is argued that manager's rather objective evaluation highly correlates with secondary data performance measures (Bauer & Anslinger, 2012, p. 217). All of the questions are closed questions, which leads to relatively structured interviews (Hollensen, 2007, p. 168) and simplifies the coding (Brymann & Bell, 2011, p. 240). Items of the constructs are measured on the basis of seven-point Likert scales. More in-depth scales, with for example nine or eleven intervals, would be impracticable for our study as managers might be unable to cope with those detailed scales (Alwin, 1997, pp. 333-334). Five-point scales, on the other, are not advisable in evaluating the post-merger phase. They are used when respondents are asked to evaluate past events (Brymann & Bell, 2011, p. 241). In fact, those five-point Likert scales are applied in section one of the questionnaire, concerning the pre-merger phase. This part however, is not subject to the study at hand and rather relates to other M&A studies having different research objectives. In order to provide a logical structure, the sections of questionnaire are installed in chronological order: Pre-merger phase, post-merger phase and

M&A performance. Section four asks for general information which is necessary for the control variables. In order to improve response rates (Brymann & Bell, 2011, p. 234), a cover letter (see Appendix B) introduces the recipient to the topic in explaining the research objective, the selection of the individual and the characteristics of the questionnaire. Furthermore, the respondent is informed about the anonymity of the data and the chance to contact the researchers in case of any questions (Brymann & Bell, 2011, p. 211). Finally, the recipients need a certain incentive to participate in the study. Therefore, the cover letter offers managers to participate in a discussion and to receipt the results after the study has been successfully terminated. Consequently, a win-win situation is created.

Pretest

In order to guarantee a successful study, a pretest has to be realized before addressing the key informants. Although all of the constructs rely on measurements models from previous studies, researchers still regard it as absolutely necessary (Hollensen, 2007, pp. 169-170) as it reduces risk of confusion and measures the time frame of the survey (Brymann & Bell, 2011, pp. 262-263). The pretest took place in February 2013 at the Management Center Innsbruck. As the pretest should be conducted by knowledgeable experts (Hollensen, 2007, p. 169), the six participants are employed in the field of academic education, banking sector and in the fields of law and economics. All of the participants were familiar with the topic of M&A and empirical studies. In first instance, the individuals responded to the questions without receiving any instructions beforehand (Brymann & Bell, 2011, p. 263). The subsequent discussion gave the participants the chance to contribute with constructive feedback.

Data Collection

The data collection started in March 2013 and ended in April 2013. At first instance, 765 questionnaires were sent out via mail. Roughly three weeks later, catch up calls were made to ensure receipt of the questionnaire. It additionally helped to collect contact details, like email addresses or telephone numbers of the key informants. The telephone calls motivated the contact persons to participate either in telephone interviews or in digital interviews realized through an online platform. As a third step, reminder emails were sent out to all of the companies in order to ensure a high participation. In total, a response rate of 18% was reached. Non-participants verified their denial with lack of time and personnel, corporate philosophy of non-participation in surveys or the departure of persons responsible for the deal. The actual respondents where CEOs, CFOs and M&A experts of the respective firm as they ought to have a global view on the M&A process (Gates & Very, 2003, p. 180)

Method of Evaluation

In the beginning of May 2013 and after eight weeks of data collection, the research team combined all of the sources of data collection in coding and recording the data into the data sheet. Incomplete datasets were repaired with a regression based method of imputation. Descriptive (describing sample) and dependent statistics (hypothesis testing) were plotted with the program SPSS. The outcome is presented and analyzed the following chapter.

4.3 Results

The following part provides an analysis of the sample of the study. It continues with the assessment of the research model. Having the basis, it is then possible to test the three hypotheses established in section 3.2.

4.3.1 Descriptive Statistics

The following part first of all analyzes the sample itself with respect to type of transaction, average industry growth, type of industry, country of buyer and target company, turnover of transaction and relative size of the target company. The study will then be tested on its reliability and validity. The latter one encompasses external as well as internal validity.

4.3.1.1 Sample Description

In total 101 respondents participated in the study, including CEOs (4%), CFOs (8%), M&A management (9%), corporate development (3%), supervisory board (6%), business managers (7%) and other positions held in the firm (7%). Unfortunately, more than half (54%) of the respondents gave no information about their position. The study involves over 101 companies from Austria, Germany and Switzerland. As it can be seen in the Figure 16, German companies were the most active ones in their transaction activities, followed by Switzerland and Austria. Some acquirers originate from other countries including CEE region, UK, USA, Italy, Japan and China. Buyer firms especially focus on national transactions. Particularly in Germany, the transactions stay within the national borders. Swiss firms tend to prefer international transactions. Preferred target firms were situated in Latin America (1), France (2), Netherlands (1), Italy (1), and Croatia (1).

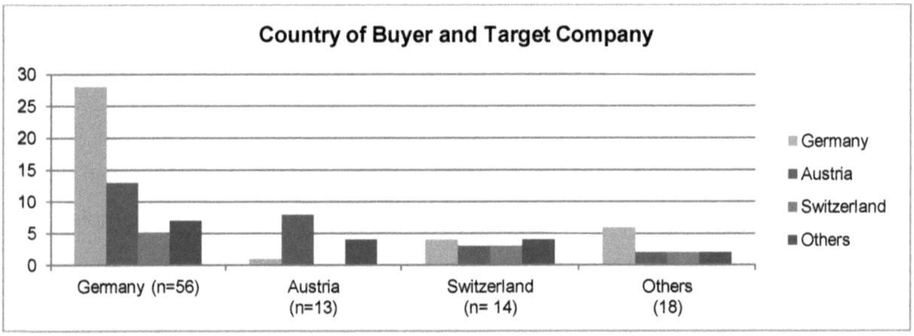

Figure 16 Country of Buyer Company and Target Company
Own elaboration according to SPSS analysis

Regarding the type of transaction, 86.67% of the companies are involved in acquisition processes. The remaining 13.33% are represented by merging transactions (see Figure 17). Horizontal transactions dominate the M&A market, followed by vertical transactions. As it can be seen in Figure 18 conglomerate transactions play a subordinate role.

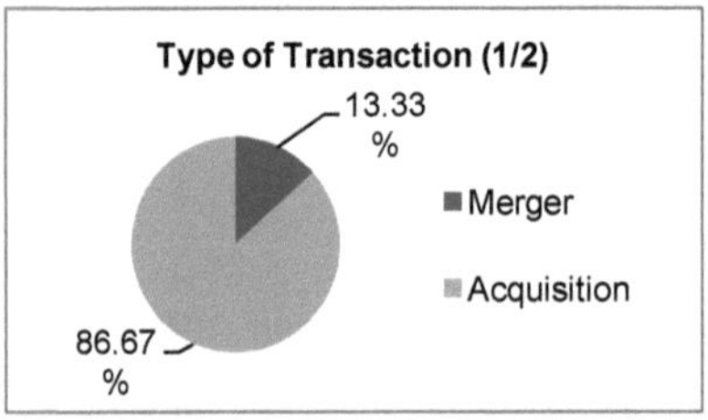

Figure 17 Type of Transaction (1/2)
Own elaboration according to SPSS analysis

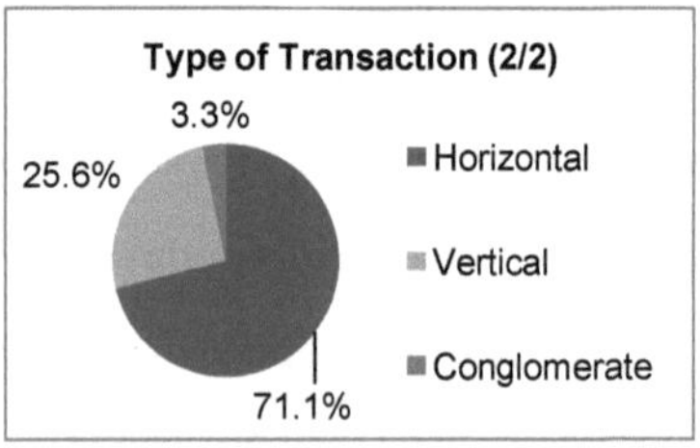

Figure 18 Type of Transaction (2/2)
Own elaboration according to SPSS analysis

As the study conducted the survey across all of the sectors, there is a relatively balanced distribution among the industries. After clustering the sample, one can see a slight majority of transaction in services, pharmaceutical industry and logistics. The segment "others" include industries like real estate or financial sector. Unfortunately, 55% did not allow for an insight in their operating industry (see Figure 19).

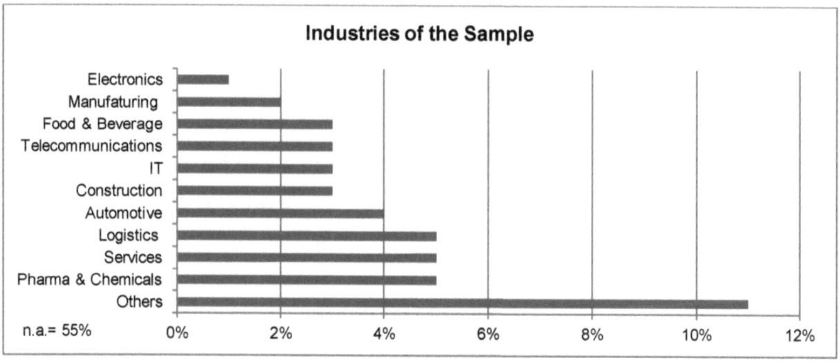

Figure 19 Industries of the Sample
Own elaboration according to SPSS analysis

Regarding the average industry growth within the previous three years before the transaction, Figure 20 outlines that the majority of the respondents evaluate a relatively low industry growth across the various segments.

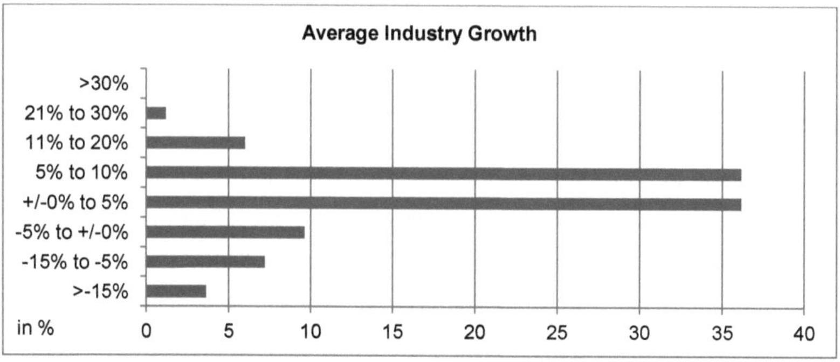

Figure 20 Average Industry Growth
Own elaboration according to SPSS analysis

In figure 21, buyer companies prefer relativly small firms. Only a few firms take the risk and acquire firms, that are double or more than the firm's own size.

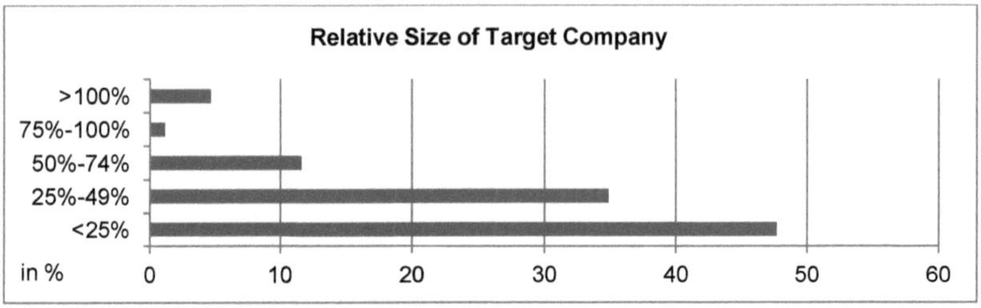

Figure 21 Relative Size of Target Company
Own elaboration according to SPSS analysis

Figure 22 shows that the turnover after the transaction mainly ranges from 100 to 249 million EUR. Surprisingly, high rates can be seen in the upper level of turnover: In fact, 14% of the companies engaged in a M&A activity realize a annual turnover higher than 1,000 million EUR.

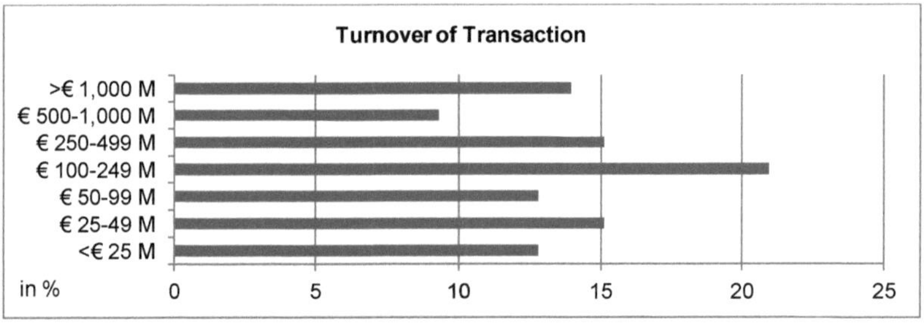

Figure 22 Relative Size of Turnover
Own elaboration according to SPSS analysis

4.3.1.2 Validity

Validity and reliability are the important terms in empirical studies. In a more narrow sense, the former one measures what should be measured while the latter one evaluates whether the data is consistent, that is stable and exact (Brymann & Bell, 2011, p. 157). The issue of reliability is described and analyzed in section 4.3.1.3. For now, the further part concentrates on the concept of validity as it is decisive for the evaluation of research results. Despite the fact that validity and reliability are different concepts, they are related as validity presumes reliability. To put it differently: If a measure is not reliable it cannot be valid (Brymann & Bell, 2011, p. 161). Generally, a research model is only valid if it does not show systematic errors (Homburg & Krohmer, 2006, p. 256). Such errors can occur internally as well as externally. External validity of research results describes the idea of whether the results of a study are universally applicable beyond the particular research concept. Therefore it is of interest to provide representative samples (Brymann & Bell, 2011, p. 43). Internal validity relates to the concept of causality and determines to what extent independent variable is at least partly responsible for the variation in the dependent variable (Brymann & Bell, 2011, p. 42). The following part tests the study at hand for first of all external and secondly internal validity.

External Validity

Late or Non-Response Bias

Late or non-response bias occurs if a certain part of the sample cannot provide the required data for several reasons (Brymann & Bell, 2011, p. 176). If such reasons are associated with the object of investigation, there might be a chance of a late or non-response bias meaning that the answers of non-respondents might deviate from the actual respondents (Klarmann, 2008, p. 286). A useful method to overcome this problem has been developed by Armstrong and Overton (1977) who assume that answers of late respondents highly correlate with answers of the non-respondents. Consequently, if the late response group does not deviate from the early respondents, there is a high probability that no late or non-response bias exists (Armstrong & Overton, 1977, pp. 399-400). The two waves of the study can be seen in the Figure 23.

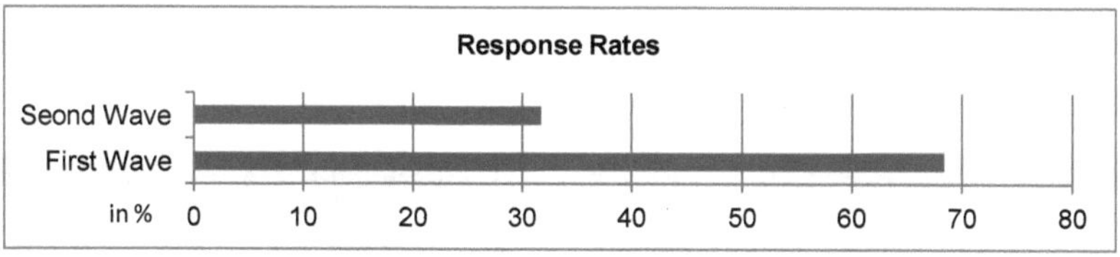

Figure 23 Response Rates According to Survey Phases
Own elaboration according to SPSS analysis

The two waves are compared with respect to the items of speed of integration. If there are no significant differences, one can argue that there exist no late or non-response bias.

Test Statistics				
	HR_Speed	Production_Speed	Marketing Speed	Systeme_Speed
Chi-Quadrat	.513	.972	.549	.49
df	1	1	1	1
Asymp. Sig.	.474	.324	.459	.825

Table 12 Kruskal-Wallis Test on Late or Non-Response Bias
Own elaboration according to SPSS analysis

As it can be taken from Table 12, there are no significant differences with regard to the two waves. Consequently, a late or non-response bias can be excluded.

Different Strokes Bias

Another source of a bias arises through the usage of different methods for conducting the survey. The present study contacted the participants through telephone, email and online platform (see Figure 24). As each of those methods stimulates different cognitive processes, the answers might differ as well (Klarmann, 2008, p. 121).

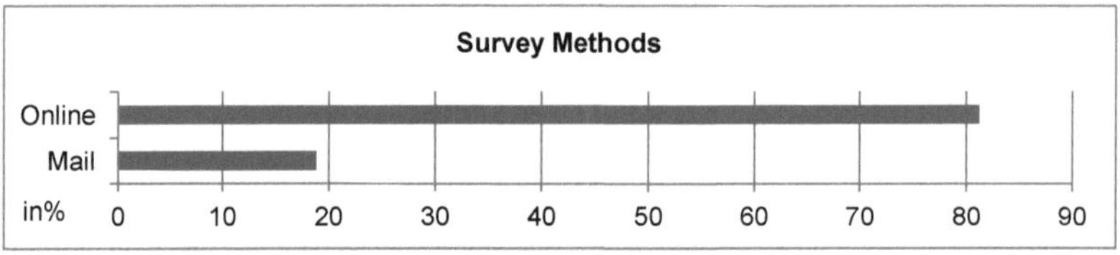

Figure 24 Survey Methods
Own elaboration according to SPSS analysis

Again, the Kruskal-Wallis test helps us to test for a different strokes bias. If the test shows significant differences amongst the methods the sample would be biased. In this case items of objective performance were used.

Test Statistics						
	Suc. obj. 1	Suc. obj. 2	Suc. obj. 3	Suc. obj 4	Suc. obj. 5	Suc. obj. 6
Chi-Quadrat	.009	.006	.041	1.258	1.561	1.367
Df	1	1	1	1	1	1
Asymp. Sig.	.926	.940	.839	.262	.212	.242

Table 13 Kruskal-Wallis Test on Different Strokes Bias
Own elaboration according to SPSS analysis

As Table 13 shows, there are no significant differences among the survey methods. Consequently, a different strokes bias can be excluded.

Item Non-Response Bias

The item non-response bias analyzes the problem of missing values within answered questionnaires, which leads to problems of interpretation and evaluation. An actual problem occurs as soon as the missing values are not random and show a certain mechanism with respect to the response behavior (Klarmann, 2008, p. 295).In order to identify a possible bias, the missing values are first of all collected. As a second step, the identified values have to be tested on whether they occur at random (Klarmann, 2008, p. 294). The investigation shows that there is no pattern behind the missing values. Therefore a non-response is not present within the data.

Non-Sampling Bias

The fourth bias that needs to be tested within the external validity is the so called non-sampling bias which describes the problem that a sample does not correspond with the actual population. A complete description of the population is usually not possible as the firm sample always depends on the availability of certain characteristics (Klarmann, 2008, p. 285). In order to detect a non-sampling bias, the characteristics of the population has to be compared with the characteristics of the sample. The following examination compares the types of transaction present in the study and the one within the population. Regarding the transaction type, the sample shows a clear tendency to more horizontal transactions (71.1%), followed by vertical (25.6%) and conglomerate (3.3%) transactions. Statistics published by the German Federal Cartel Office show that in 2007 and 2008, companies that conducted horizontal acquisitions by far exceeded the number of vertical acquisitions or conglomerates. To be more precise, in 2008, 1,341 horizontal acquisitions and only 92 vertical transactions have been realized (Glaum & Hutzschenreuter, 2010, p. 21).To sum it up, the sample within this study harmonizes with the population characteristics. As a result, it is likely that a non-sampling bias does not exist within this study.

Internal Validity

Common Method Bias

The common method bias describes a serious problem of behavioral research, as it biases the variance and covariance of the data. Such a bias exists if the dependent and independent variable are measured with one single instrument (Klarmann, 2008, p. 156). The common method bias variance is one of the main sources of measurement errors and describes the "variance that is attributable to the measurement method rather than to the constructs the measures represent" (Podsakoff, MacKenzie, Lee, & Podsakoff, 2003, p. 879). In order to identify whether such a bias has occurred within the study I make use of the Harman's single factor test, presented by Podsakoff and colleagues (Podsakoff, MacKenzie, Lee, & Podsakoff, 2003, p. 889). It is measured whether all items used in this study form one method factor. Relying on Harman's Single factor test all items are measured on more than one factor (see Appendix A). Consequently, a common method bias can be excluded.

Key Informant Bias

In contrast to the common method bias, the key informant bias depends on the interviewed individuals. In course of the survey conducted among key informants, there is a chance of a bias with respect to variance and covariance within the data (Podsakoff, MacKenzie, Lee, & Podsakoff, 2003, p. 886). Consequently, the reliability regarding information of relevant characteristics is questioned (Podsakoff, MacKenzie, Lee, & Podsakoff, 2003, p. 887). For testing the bias, I compare the performance evaluated by the top level management with the one from the market data. If both figures highly harmonize, a key informant bias can be excluded. According to the study, 43% evaluate the overall M&A performance as negative. This number corresponds to the widely accepted assumption that on average 40-60% of M&A transactions fail to create value (Cartwright & Cooper, 1995,p. 33; Jansen, 2001, p. 240). Despite the tendency of similar figures, a key informant bias cannot be completely excluded.

Summarizing the findings, it can be said that the data provides internal as well as external validity. Referring on the later one, late or non-response bias and different strokes bias were disproved by applying the Kruskal-Wallis test.

Item non-response bias as well as non-sampling bias pose no problem either. Internal validity was proven by the non existence of common method bias and the key informant bias. The later one will be analyzed in more details in section 5.3.

4.3.1.3 Reliability

As stated in section 4.3.1.2, validity presumes reliability (Brymann & Bell, 2011, p. 161) . Therefore it is of utmost importance to check the data on its reliability that is to prove the consistence of the data. Table 14 provides an overview of the items and the respective loadings.

Item and Construct Reliability						
Construct		Items	Factor loading > 0.707		Cronbach's α > 0.7	
Human integration		Organizational structure	.830		.824	
		Organizational culture	.863			
		HR management	.886			
Task integration	Production integration	Production	.741	.877	.726	.764
		Supply sources	.747			
	Marketing integration	Distribution channels	.805	.855	.847	
		Sales/after-sales service	.823			
		Marketing programs	.782			
	System integration	Strategic planning systems	.792	.736	.841	
		Financial and budget systems	.880			
		Mgmt information systems	.853			
Task integration duration		Production integration	.736		.712	
		Marketing integration	.812			
		System integration	.843			
Task integration speed		Production integration	.764		.724	
		Marketing integration	.835			
		System integration	.811			
M&A performance	Subjective M&A performance	Goals set have been reached	.899	.918	.899	.801
		Optimal business decision	.890			
		Acquisition was a success	.872			
		Company performs better now	.848			

	Objective M&A performance	Return on investment	.900	.918	.918	
		Return on equity	.869			
		Return on sales	.869			
		Enterprise value	.868			
		Turnover	.803			
		Market share	.756			

Table 14 Test on Reliability
Own elaboration according to SPSS analysi

Apparent from the testing, all factor loadings onto their corresponding constructs met the conditions of x>0.707 and show a high significance, indicating a high degree of individual item reliability. Therefore, item reliability is proven. Regarding the construct liability, all the constructs show a value $\alpha > 0.7$, where the lowest value amounts to 0.712. Combining the items and construct liability, it is proven that the analyzed data is stable and exact. The measurement model is therefore acceptable.

4.3.2 Evaluation of the Research Model

Table 15 represents the correlation matrix of all constructs and single items measures applied in this study with the respective mean values and standard deviations.

		1.	2.	3.	4.	5.	6.	7.	8.
1.	Task integration speed	1	--	--	--	--	--	--	--
2.	Human integration speed	.489**	1	--	--	--	--	--	--
3.	Difference human integration speed - task integration speed	-.347**	.648**	1	--	--	--	--	--
4.	Relative size	-.004	-.162	-.173	1	--	--	--	--
5.	Industry growth	.057	-.057	-.115	.169	1	--	--	--
6.	Annual turnover	-.121	-.033	.073	.065	-.052	1	--	--
7.	Type of transaction (2/2)	-.199	-.287**	-.130	-.144	-.193	-.026	1	--
8.	Transaction Experience	.054	.075	.033	-.168	-.057	.293**	-.110	1
	Mean value	3.1884	2.6933	-.4951	1.80	4.17	3.94	1.32	2.73
	Standard deviation	1.32516	1.63174	1.51734	1.015	1.188	1.924	.537	1.297

Table 15 Correlation Matrix
Own elaboration according to SPSS analysis result

The results of my regression analysis show that the control variables have, to some extent, an influence on our research model. Table 16 provides the results of the regression analysis including ß-value and significance of each construct as well as the overall F-value and R square.

	Effects on Performance (3 to 5 years after the transaction)		
	Model 1	Model 2	Model 3
Task integration speed	--	-.231+	--
Human integration speed	--	.365**	--
Difference human integration speed - task integration speed	--	--	.304**
Control variables:			
Relative size	.041	.107	.100
Industry growth	.182	.212+	.213+
Annual turnover	.072	.043	.035
Type of transaction (2/2)	-.097	-.004	-.027
Transaction experience	.205+	.205+	.211+
F-value	1.688	2.420*	2.777*
R-square adjusted	.042	.112	.119

Table 16 Evaluation of Model 1, 2 and 3
Own elaboration according to SPSS analysis result

Model 1: As a first step, I analyzed the controls as a baseline. Regressing the controls relative size (ß=0.41; n.s.), industry growth (ß=0.182; n.s.) and annual turnover (ß=0.072; n.s.), on M&A performance results in a non significant relationship. Also type of transaction (2/2), that is horizontal, vertical or conglomerate (ß=-.097; n.s.), shows no significance. However, the transaction experience has a positive influence on M&A performance on a 10% level (ß=.205; $p \leq 0.1$) with a moderate ß-value. As apparent from the table, adjusted R square, that is the amount of variance for a dependent variable, shows a moderate value (R^2=0.042) meaning that the model explains the dependent variable. The F-value is not significant (F-Value=1.731; n.s.), however, one can expect the value to be significant with an increasing number of participants.

Model 2: Model 2 regresses the M&A performance on control variables and direct effects. The control variables relative size (ß=0.107; n.s.), annual turnover (ß=0.043; n.s.) and type of transaction (2/2) (ß=-.097; n.s.) are no significant predictors for the M&A performance. However, in terms of industry growth (ß=.212; $p \leq 0.1$), we obtain a positive regression coefficient. Transaction experience (ß=.205; $p \leq 0.1$) remains to have moderate positive effect. It furthermore indicates that task integration speed (ß=-.231; $p \leq 0.1$) has negative effect on M&A performance. In contrast, human integration speed shows (ß=0.365; $p \leq .01$) a strong positive significant effect on M&A performance. This time, the model was able to explain 11.2% (R^2=0.112) of the variance of the dependent variable. The presented F-value explains the model on a significant level (F-Value=1.731; $p \leq 0.1$).

Model 3: Model 3 provides evidence for the difference effect of speed which is explained by subtracting task integration speed from human integration speed. The independent variable (ß=.304; $p \leq 0.01$) shows a strong positive effect at a 1% level. The control variables industry growth (ß=.213; $p \leq 0.1$) and transaction experience (ß=.211; $p \leq 0.1$) remain to significantly influence M&A performance in a positive way. The R square here shows that we are able to explain 11.9% of the variance of the dependent variable which is a satisfying value. As the F-value shows a significant effect on a 5% level (F-value= 2.777; $p \leq 0.05$), the model satisfies the criteria.

4.3.3 Hypotheses Testing

Based on the path coefficients and significance outlined in the previous section this part evaluates the three hypotheses (see Figure 25). After the evaluation, the respective hypothesis is either rejected or accepted.

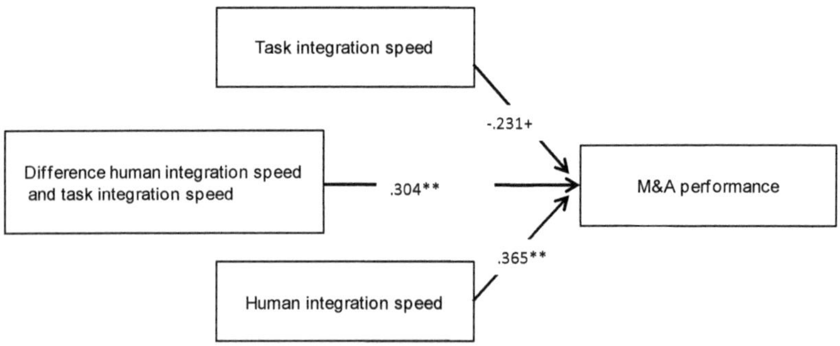

Figure 25 Research Model Results
Own elaboration according to SPSS analysis

The first hypothesis determined the effect of task integration speed on the M&A performance. As proposed, the independent variable task integration speed has a moderate negative effect with ß=-.231+ on M&A performance. However, I argue that with an increasing sample the significance would increase as well. Consequently, the first hypothesis can be accepted. This finding contradicts study results of various studies, as for example Angwin (2004) and Schlaepfer and colleagues (2008), who support the idea that the first 100 days are essential for task integration and M&A performance. (Angwin, 2004, p. 428; Schlaepfer et al., 2008, p. 9). However, the findings are in line with the previous study results of Bauer and colleagues (2013) as well as Birkinshaw and colleagues (2000) who found an also a negative effect of a fast task integration with respect to M&A performance (Bauer et al., 2013, p. 6; Birkinshaw, 2000, p. 419). Within the second hypothesis I argued that cultural integration speed has an opposite effect as compared to task integration speed. I assumed that a fast cultural integration promotes the M&A success. Apparent from the regression analysis presented in the previous part, the independent variable cultural integration speed has a strong positive effect with ß= .365** on M&A performance. Again, this finding is in line with study results of Bauer and colleagues (2013) as well as Birkinshaw and colleagues (2000) who argue for a fast human integration in order to promote M&A success (Bauer et al., 2013, p. 6; Birkinshaw, 2000, p. 420).

Combining hypothesis one and two, the third hypothesis reasons that human integration has to be integrated faster than task integration. In other words: There has to be a difference between human integration speed and task integration speed that positively influences M&A performance. The results show a strong positive relationship between the independent variable and M&A performance with a high value of ß= .304**. Consequently, the hypothesis can be confirmed and it can be concluded that the human integration process facilitates the task integration process which in turn fosters M&A performance. Up until now, this finding has not been quantitatively proven by any researcher. However it underlines the assumptions made by Birkinshaw and colleagues (2000) who argue that a high level of human integration promotes the effectiveness of task integration which in turn forces the M&A success (Birkinshaw et al., 2000, p.

419). In line with this assumption, Bauer and colleagues (2013) argue that the benefits of human integration already in place outweigh the costs of forgoing a fast synergy realization (Bauer et al., 2013, p.7).

4.4 Summary of Results

My key theoretical argument was that human factors have to be integrated before task integration. Consistent with those assumptions, I find that task integration speed negatively influences the M&A performance, while the opposite effect can be observed with respect to human integration speed. All of the tested hypotheses deliver significant results. The first hypothesis can be accepted as the data provides evidence that slow task integration increases M&A success. The second important insight confirms results of previous studies and argues that the faster culture and human beings are integrated the more likely the company will successfully perform the overall transaction. The most striking and logically observation that results from the preceding observations is that the M&A performance increases if human integration is relatively faster than task integration. In other words, human integration pursued before task integration facilitates the whole process, because individuals on both sides do know each other and consequently trust each other. The evaluations of the control variables shows that mainly industry growth and transaction experience have a positive influence on the dependent variable of M&A performance. Companies operating in a growing industry sector show a better M&A performance than those operating in consistent or shrinking industry sectors. It can be furthermore observed that with an increasing experience in transactions, companies increase their M&A success.

5 Discussion

Built on the previous results of the study the last chapter provides a profound insight of managerial and theoretical implications. As a last step, the limitations with respect to the study method and content are outlined. This part also contains further research suggestions in order to minimize the limitations occurred within the study.

5.1 Managerial Implications

Despite managerial awareness of speed in post-merger integration (Glaum & Hutzschenreuter, 2010, p. 211), M&A literature has almost ignored its potential positive influence on M&A performance. Relying on this assumption, the research model at hand sheds light into the dark and outlines the importance of speed of integration for management activities which determines M&A success or failure. With this study, managers receive scientific evidence on which they can ground their future activities and decisions. The outcomes clarify the managerial question of whether speed of integration is beneficial or not. The answer cannot be generally answered with a simple yes or no. Therefore I established a way to identify the correct speed in separating the integration process into task integration and human integration. In simple terms I replaced the question "Is speed of integration beneficial to M&A success" with "Which type of speed of integration is beneficial for M&A success?". In fact, I found that the pace of integration depends on the type of integration. Consequently it can be said, that human integration has to be integrated faster than task integration. This study enhances the under researched topic of speed of integration and widens practical implications in essentially three ways:

The first outcome contrasts the arguments of a majority of M&A researchers who opt for fast task integration. According to Angwin (2004) for example, managers should make use of the "window of opportunity" and benefit from the early enthusiasm of stakeholders (Angwin, 2004, p. 420). Being concerned with their responsibilities, employees may only focus on their specific task rather than on the overall M&A task, that is combining the responsibilities of the two firms. Based on the credo of Chase (1998) that there are "three things that matter the most here, and they are speed, speed, speed" (Chase, 1998, p.3), it is widely assumed that capabilities should be transferred quickly in order decrease cost and increase the competitive advantage. However, my study shows that slow task integration and the step by step transfer of capabilities and knowledge transfer increases subjective and objective M&A performance. Consequently, managers are well advised to distribute responsibilities to all employees, both from the buyer and target firm, within a moderate time frame. By integrating the task in a consistent way, managers are able to control the process and reduce possible conflicts with respect to unit crossing or employees.

The second implication provides for an advanced understanding for managers with respect to human integration that clearly asks for high speed of integration. This finding is of utmost importance as it once more underpins the importance of culture and encourages managers to take action within the cultural integration activities. In contrast to the case of task integration, the "window of opportunity" (Angwin, 2004, p. 420) here seems to be a reasonable argument for a fast integration. By converging the culture of the target company and the culture of the buyer company, the managers should make use of the early enthusiasm of the employees. Therefore, trust can be encouraged, physical and mental illness is reduced to a minimum where especially merger stress syndrome will not have a chance to take place. Managers may reach this relatively early human integration through effective communication that should start within the pre-merger phase and may continue throughout the whole M&A process. No matter which action is taken by the managers, they have to be aware of the complex field of culture.

The most striking implication of this study is the fact that it has been quantitatively proven that human integration facilitates task integration, as the overall performance increased with a faster integration of culture. Managers should be aware of their own managerial resources with respect to time and money. Task and human integration are different processes that have to be considered equally. Depending on the integration type managers have to focus on different actions and objectives. Task integration asks for combining and eliminating operation in order to achieve synergies while human integration builds an atmosphere of mutual trust and respect to create employee satisfaction (Birkinshaw et al. 2000, p. 400). It sounds intuitively logical, that concentrating on both complex processes seems quite challenging and might lead to a decreased performance outcome. Therefore, priorities have to be set. In fact, I recommend to first of all building a solid cultural basis on which employees trust each other, share ideas and knowledge. Having set this fundament, managers can build on this process and put more effort into task integration, however, without completely ignoring cultural integration. Evaluating cost and benefits of the pace of integration, managers will realize that the benefits of a fast human integration will outweigh the costs for slow task integration. I argue that integrating culture first will result in a long-term stable M&A relationship and overall success.

Having provided a guideline to decide on whether to integrate fast or slow, I suggest to still outweighing costs and benefits of fast or slow integration. Combing the findings, managers are well advised to handle their individual resources efficiently and concentrate on one thing after the other rather than simultaneously implementing all processes.

Besides the human integration speed and task integration speed, two factors have influenced the M&A performance as well, that are industry growth and transaction experience. Therefore, companies operating in a highly growing industry sector outperform the ones operating in shrinking industry sectors. Furthermore, managers who realized various transactions in the past are more likely to be successful in the integration process than the one with no or limited experience. Another factor I have identified was the influence of transaction experience on task and human integration speed: With an increasing transaction experience the relative speed of integration increases as well. The effect diminishes as soon as companies have conducted more than five transactions beforehand. In fact, the overall integration speed decreases. To put it short: A converted u-shaped curve exists. Consequently, I argue that managers may not solely rely on their transaction experience.

5.2 Theoretical Implications

The study contributes not only to the world of practical M&A management, it furthermore enhances the field of scientific M&A research. The following part outlines the main implications with respect to speed and human integration in M&A science.

Consideration of Speed of Integration within M&A Research

The study gives voice to the under researched topic of speed of integration within the M&A literature and adds to a topic in process school of thought. As demonstrated in 2.3.1, a moderate growing body of literature and studies tried to identify the interrelation of speed on integration and the M&A success. Up to know no single study quantitatively identified the different paces of integration in terms of the different organizational levels. The study contributes to the suggestion of Bauer and Anslinger (2012) who argue that the complex topic of speed of integration cannot be demonstrated in one single model (Bauer & Anslinger, 2012, p. 219). In fact, there have to be several studies that combine the overall findings which in turn lead to a profound understanding. This specific model contributes to the suggested collection of models. The study furthermore provides evidence that speed cannot be regarded isolated and that deterministic factors have to be taken into consideration. The control variable transaction experience, for example, shows a converted u-shaped curve in terms of speed of integration. Despite the fact that studies already started to evaluate the deterministic factor within the speed of integration, further investigations are absolutely necessary. A third advancement that has been made refers to the measurement model and its calculation of the two independent variables task integration speed and human integration speed. The proposed model by Bauer (2012) suggesting calculating relative speed of integration rather than the absolute speed of integration (Bauer & Matzler, 2012, p. 17), has proven to be a useful and effective measure. I can therefore argue that compared to previous studies, the present one provides more conclusive results as the formula decreases volatility and reliability.

Consideration of Human Integration within M&A Research

Despite the fact that M&A literature is still concerned with mostly financial and market studies (Cartwright & Schoenberg, 2006, p. 1) , the present study verifies that human integration is of essential importance. The combination of two complex topics within M&A research, that is human integration and speed of integration have shown that it has a significant importance with respect to M&A success. Consequently, considering human integration speed paves the way into a new relatively unexplored field of M&A research.

5.3 Limitations and Future Research

The study presents various implications and suggestions for M&A management and scientist. However, it is also restricted to limitations. The following part outlines limitations with regards to the methods and content. Combing the implications and limitations, the last part of the paper provides an outlook and future research suggestion.

5.3.1 Methodological Limitations

Within the study, survey related problems have to be taken into consideration. Based on the biases analyzed in section 4.3.1.2 the following part outlines the main limitations with respect to methodology. As the survey was conducted among individuals the most significant issue refers to the key informant bias. It is assumed that individuals lose their ability to memorize past events (Golden, 1992, p. 848) and decrease their capacity of recollections (Sudman & Bradburn, 1973) in course of time. Consequently, retrospective errors occur (Golden, 1992, p. 848). This bias cannot be eliminated totally and there will always be a gap between reliable data and limited capacity of recollection. A further limitation, that arises with all self-reports, is a potential common method bias (Podsakoff, MacKenzie, Lee, & Podsakoff, 2003, p. 889). Despite the fact that the Harman's single factor test, conducted in sections 4.3.1.2, indicates no serious problem, the bias cannot be excluded completely. The third limitation arises with the restriction of the sample collection that encompasses the position of respondents, geographical area and time period. Following the suggestion of Bauer and Anslinger (2012), I argue that it might be beneficial to extend the individuals questioned (Bauer & Anslinger, 2012, p. 217). My survey relies on exclusively top management and collects their professional opinion. However, there are much more individuals involved in the transaction process which voices should be heard. An additional limitation arises from the geographical aspect of the survey. Data was collected in DACH region which only allows for the reflection on specific management cultures and employee behavior. The level of uncertainty, perception and stress factor of people might be different in Asia or in the US (Homburg & Bucerius, 2006, p. 364). Therefore I suggest conducting the study countries with different cultural background. With respect to the measurement model, future research could improve the measurement model or to extent it. Up to now, external effects like economic crises or political forces were partly ignored. Referring to the measurement model, it would be advisable to reshape the construct measurements and go beyond the suggested measurements of Becker (2005) and Cording et al. (2008). The construct measurement of human integration, for example, is limited the organizational structure, organizational culture and HR management practices (Cording et al., 2008, p. 751). It is questionable whether the degree of integration measured by those items reflects the actual ability of the firm to overcome merger stress, anxiety or pressure of its employees. The measurement of human integration could be extended by factors that were implemented in other successful studies. Visibility and continuity of leadership or the communication process during the integration process, dimension used by Birkinshaw et al. (2000), might be of interest in future studies (Birkinshaw et al., 2000, p. 413).

5.3.2 Content Limitations

Next to the methodological limitations are mainly two limitations with regards to the content. Firstly, I did not explore the interplay of speed and other success factors. The control variable of transaction experience already showed that speed is influenced by various factors. Other factors like relatedness or cultural compatibly could increase the significance of performance effects (Bauer & Anslinger, 2012, p. 218). Secondly, I only focus on the post-merger integration. The M&A process however should be regarded as a holistic approach (Bauer & Matzler, 2013, p. 1) as only this allows for a sufficient evaluation of M&A performance.

5.3.3 Future Research

In general, future research is needed in the area of speed of integration and more concrete in the field of human integration speed and task integration speed. With respect to human integration, studies have been established and more consideration was taken on the human aspects in M&A activities. However, the topic culture is very complex and further studies should quantitatively focus on human integration speed and its influencing factors. Which variables could foster the speed of cultural integration and which variables hinder the speed? Considering task integration speed, there are various studies promoting a fast integration. Relying on the findings of the study, future research may discover more arguments for a slow integration of tasks by and quantitatively proving positive effects on M&A performance and additional dependent variables. Generally, future studies could examine the effects of speed of integration with respect to M&A performance, which do not have to be necessarily linear but may occur in non-linear effects as for example an inverted u-shaped curve.

Additionally, all of the above mentioned limitations provide a basis for further research. To be more precise, geographical limitations could be overcome as outcome effects may differ from culture to culture. Therefore, future research could go beyond the DACH region and make the M&A concept more globally acceptable. Furthermore, respondents should be at least employees or customers and not limited to top management. The performance evaluation might differ but might provide more precise findings. Additionally, studies with respect to speed of integration should apply a more holistic approach and integrate the pre-merger and transaction phase. As control variables seem to influence M&A performance and speed of integration, they should receive more attention. The transaction experience has already been explored, however I suggest that other controls like company size or industry growth could be taken into consideration. Finally, as already mentioned within the limitations, improved measurement models with respect to human integration and task integration might be a next step into a successful M&A analysis.

Bibliography

Alwin, D. F. (1997). Feeling thermometers versus 7-point scales – which are better? *Sociological Methods Research , 25* (3), pp. 318-340.

Angwin, D. (2007). Motive archetypes in merger and acquisitions (M&A): The imploications of a configurational approach to performance. In S. F. Cary L. Cooper, *Advances in mergers and acquisitions* (6 ed., pp. 77–105). Amsterdam: Elsevier Ltd.

Angwin, D. (2004). Speed in M&A integration: The first 100 days. *European Management Journal , 22* (4), pp. 418-430.

Appelbaum, S., Gandell, J., Yortis, A., Proper, S., & Jobin, F. (2000). Anatomy of a merger: Behavior of organizational factors and processes thoughout the pre-during-post stages . *Management Decision , 38* (9), pp. 649-661.

Armstrong, S. J., & Overton, T. S. (1977). Estimating nonresponse bias in mail surveys. *Journal of Marketing Research , XIV*, pp. 396-402.

Balz, U., & Arlinghaus, O. (2007). *Praxisbuch Mergers & Acquisitions.* Landsberg am Lech: mi_Fachverlag.

Bauer, F. (2012). *Integratives M&A Management.* Wiesbaden: Gabler Verlag.

Bauer, F., & Anslinger, T. (2012). Kognitive Beschleunigung oder affektive Entschleunigung? Zur Rolle der Integrationsgeschwindigkeit bei M&A. In I. Saenger, & G. Schewe, *Forum Mergers & Acquisitions 2012* (pp. 210-220). Wiesbaden: Gabler Research/ Springer Fachmedien.

Bauer, F., & Matzler, K. (2013). Antecents of the M&A success: The role of strategic complementarity, cultural fit and degree and speed of integration. *Strategic Management Journal , doi: 10. 1002/smj.2091*, pp. 1-23.

Bauer, F., & Matzler, K. (2012). Developing a better measure for speed of integration. *Proceedings of the EURAM 2013, Istanbul* , pp. 1-22.

Bauer, F., & Matzler, K. (2011). Developing a more holistic understanding of M&A - Connecting schools of thought and phases of the M&A process through insights from central European SME transactions. *Porceedings to the EURAM 2011* , pp. 1-41.

Bauer, F., Degischer, D., & Matzler, K. (2013). Is speed of integration learnable? *Proceedings of the Make Learn Conference 2013* , pp. 1-9.

Becker, D. R. (2005). *Ressourcen-Fit bei M&A-Transaktionen.* Wiesbaden: Deutscher Universitaets-Verlag.

Behringer, S. (2013). *Unternehmenstransaktionen.* Berlin: Erich Schmidt Verlag.

Bell, J. (1996). *Single or joint venturing? A comprehensive approach to foreign.* Surrey: Avebury.

Berdie, D. R., & Anderson, J. F. (1976). Mail questionnaire response rates: Updating outmoded thinking. *Journal of Marketing , 40* (1), pp. 71-73.

Beth-von der Warth, A. (2004). *Personalarbeit bei Merger & Acquisitions.* Duesseldorf: Hans-Boeckler-Stiftung.

Bijlsma-Frankema, K. (2001). On managing cutural integration and cultural change processes in mergers and acquisitions. *Journal of European Industrial Training , 25*, pp. 192-207.

Birkinshaw, J., Bresman, H., & Hakanson, L. (2000). Manageing the post acquisition integration process: How human integration and task integration processes interact to foster value creation. *Journal of Management Studies , 37* (3), pp. 365-425.

Birkinshaw, J., Bresman, H., & Hakanson, L. (2000, Vol. 37 Nr. 3). Manageing the post acqusition intergration process: How human integration and task integration processes interact to foster value creation. *Journal of Management Studies* , pp. 395-425.

Bloomberg. (2013, May). *Deutsche Boerse AG German Stock Index DAX.* Retrieved May 27, 2013, from http://www.bloomberg.com/quote/DAX:IND

Boland, R. (1970). How much weight do personel factors carry? *Personnel , 47*, 8-13.

Bradley, F. (2005). *International Marketing Strategy* (5 ed.). Essex: Pearson Education Limited.

Bragado, & Fuster, J. (1992). Setting the correct speed for postmerger integration. *M&A Europe , 5*, pp. 24-31.

Brähler, G. (2008). *Umwandlungssteuerrecht – Grundlagen für Studium und Steuerpruefung* (4 ed.). Wiesbaden: Springer Gabler Verlag.

Bresman, H., Brikinshaw, J., & Nobel, R. (2010). Knowledge transfer in internation acquisitions. *Journal of International Business Studies , 41*, 5-20.

Brymann, A., & Bell, E. (2011). *Business research mehtods* (3 ed.). Oxford: Oxford University Press.

Buono, A. F., & Bowditch, J. L. (2003). *The human side of mergers and acquisitions: Managing collisions between people, cultures and organizations.* Washington, D. C.

Calipha, R., Tarba, S., & Brock, D. (2010). Mergers and acquisitions: A review of phases, motives, and success factors. In S. Finkelstein, & C. L. Cooper, *Advances in merger and acquisitions* (9 ed., pp. 1-24). Bingley: Emerald.

Campbell, A., & Goold, M. (1998). Desperatly seeking synergy. *Harvard Business Review , 76*, 131-146.

Capasso, A., & Meglio, O. (2005). Knowledge transfer in mergers and acquisitions: How frequent acquirers learn to manage the integration process. In A. Capasso, G. B. Dagnino, & A. Lanza, *Strategic capabilities and knowledge transfer within and between organizations* (pp. 199-225). Northampton.

Capron, L., & Pistre, N. (2002). When do acquirers earn abnormal returns? *Strategic Management Journal , 23*, pp. 294-312.

Cartwright, S. (2005). Mergers and acquisitions: An update and appraisal. *International Review of Industrial and Organizational Psychology , 20*, pp. 1-38.

Cartwright, S., & Cooper, G. L. (1995). Organizational marriage: "hard" versus "soft" issues? *Personnel Review , 24* (3), pp. 31-42.

Cartwright, S., & Schoenberg, R. (2006). Thity years of mergers and acquisitions research: Recent advances and future opportunities. *British Journal of Management , 17*, pp. 1-5.

Chanmugam, R., Shill, W., Mann, D., Ficery, K., & Pursche, B. (2005). The intelligent clean room: ensuring value. *Journal of Business Strategy , 26*, pp. 43-49.

Chase, B. (1998). National city´s latest mergers put premium on fast executuion. *American banker , 163*, pp. 3-4.

Chatterjee, S., Lubatkin, M. H., Schweiger, D. M., & Weber, Y. (1992). Cultural differences and shareholder value in related mergers: Linking equity and human capital. *Strategic Management Journal , 13* (5), 319-334.

Christensen, C. M., Alton, R., Rising, C., & Waldeck, A. (2011, March). The new M&A playbook. *Harvard Business Review* , pp. 48-57.

Colombo, G., Conca, V., Buongiorno, M., & Gnan, L. (2007). Integrating cross-border acquisitions: A process oriented approach. *Long Range Planning , 40*, pp. 202-222.

Colquitt, J. A., Wesson, M. J., Porter, C. O., & Yee, K. N. (2001). Justice at the millenium: A meta-analytic review of 25 years of organizational justice research. *Journal of Applied Psychology , 86* (3), pp. 425-445.

Cording, M., Christman, P., & King, D. R. (2008). Reducing causal ambiguity in acquisition integration: Intermediate goals as mediators of integration decision and acquisition performance. *Academy of Management Journal , 51* (4), pp. 744-767.

Creed, D. W., & Miles, R. E. (1996). Trust in organizations: A conceptual framework. In R. M. Kramer, & T. R. Tyler, *Trust in organizations: Frontiers of theory and research* (pp. 16-38). London: Sage.

Darr, E. D., & Kurtzberg, T. R. (2000). An investigation of partner similarity dimensions in knowledge transfer. *Organizational Behavior and Human Decision Process , 82*, pp. 28-44.

Datta, D. K. (1991). Organizational fit and acquisition performance: Effects on post acquisition integration. *Strategic Management Journal , 12* (4), pp. 281-297.

DeLong, G. (2003). The announcement effects of U.S. versus non-U.S. bank mergers: Do they differ? *The journal of Financial Research , XXVI* (4), 487-500.

DeMeuse, K. P. (1987). Corporate surgery: The human trauma of mergers and acquisitions. *95th annual meeting of the American Psychological Association.* New York.

Depamphilis, D. M. (2010). *Mergers, acquisitions, and other restructuring activities: An integrated approach to process, tools, cases, and solutions.* Burlington: Academic Press.

Diekmann, A. (2006). *Grundlagen, Methoden, Anwendungen, Empirische Sozialforschung* (17 ed.). Berlin: Rowolth.

Drumm, H. J. (1991). Probleme der Erfassung und Messung von Unternehmenskultu. In E. Dülfer, *Organisationskultur.* Stuttgart: Schäffer-Poeschel Verlag.

Duchin, R., & Schmid, B. (2013). Riding the merger wave: Uncertainty, reduced monitoring, and bad acquisitions. *Journal of Financial Economics , 107* (1), pp. 69-88.

Ebster, C. (1999). *Martforschung leicht gemacht: Wettebewerbsvorsprung durch Information.* Wien: Ueberreuter.

Elsass, P. M., & Veiga, J. (1994). Acculturation in acquired organizations:A force-field perspective. *Human Relations , 47*, pp. 431–453.

Empson, L. (2004). Organizational identity change: Managerial regulation and member identification in an accounting firm acquisition. *Accounting, Organizations and Society , 29*, pp. 759-781.

Epstein, M. J. (2004). The drivers of success in post-merger integration. *Organizational Dynamics , 33* (2), pp. 174-189.

European Central Bank, I. (2013, May). *European Central Bank Eurosystem*. Retrieved May 27, 2013, from http://www.ecb.europa.eu/stats/monetary/rates/html/index.en.html

Finkelstein, S., & Cooper, C. L. (2010). *Advances in mergers and aquisitions* (9 ed.). Bingley: Emerald .

Gadiesh, O., Ormiston, C., & Rovit, S. (2003). Achieving an M&A´s strategic goals at maximum speed for maximum value. *Strategy & Leadership , 31* (3), pp. 35-41.

Gambetta, D. (1988). Can we trust? In D. Gambetta, *Trust: Making and breaking corporate relations* (pp. 213-237). Oxford: Basil Blackwell.

Gates, S., & Very, P. (2003). Measuring performance during M&A integration. *Long Range Planning , 36*, pp. 167-185.

Gerds, J., & Schewe, G. (2004). *Post Merger Integration – Unternehmenserfolg durch Integration Excellence.* Berlin.

Gerpott, T. J. (1993). *Integrationsgestaltung und Erfolg von Unternehmensakquisitionen.* Stuttgart.

Glaum, M., & Hutzschenreuter, T. (2010). *Mergers and Acquisitions: Management des externen Unternehmenswachstums.* Stuttgart: W. Kohlhammer GmbH.

Glaum, M., Lindemann, J., & Friedrich, N. (2006). Erfolg von Mergers & Acquisitions – Ergebnisse einer empirischen Forschung. In B. Wirtz, *Handbuch Mergers & Acquisitions Management* (pp. 287-314). Wiesbaden: Gabler.

Golden, B. R. (1992). The past is the past--or is it? The use of retrospective accounts as indicators of past strategy. *The Academy of Management Journal , 35* (4), 848-860.

Gorzala, J. (2010). *The art of hostile takeover.* Hamburg: Igel-Verlag.

Habeck, M. M., Kröger, F., & Träm, M. (2002). *Wi(e)der das Fusionsfieber –Die sieben Schlüsselfaktoren erfolgreicher Fusionen, 2. Aufl., Wiesbaden* (2 ed.). Wiesbaden: Gabler Verlag.

Halebian, J., & Finkelstein, S. (1999). The influence of organizational acquisition experience on acquisition performance: A behavioural learning perspective. *Administrative Science Quarterly , 44*, pp. 29-56.

Harford, J. (2005). What drives merger waves? *Journal of Financial Economics , 77*, pp. 529-560.

Haspeslagh, P. C., & Jemison, D. B. (1991). *Akquisitionsmanagement: Wertschoepfung durch strategische Neuausrichtung des Unternehmens.* New York: The Free Press.

Hermalin, B. E. (2001). Economics and corporate culture. In C. L. Cooper, S. Cartwright, & C. P. Earley, *Handbook of Organizational Culture* (pp. 217-262). Chichester, U.K.: John Wiley and Sons.

Hogg, M. A., & Terry, D. J. (2000). Social identity and self-categorization processes in organizational contexts. *Academic Management Revue , 25*, pp. 121-140.

Hollensen, S. (2007). *Global marketing: A decison-oriented approach* (4 ed.). Essex: Pearson Educated Limited.

Homburg, C., & Bucerius, M. (2005). A marketing perspective on mergers and acquisitions: How marketing integration affects postmerger performance. *Journal of Marketing , 69*, pp. 95–113.

Homburg, C., & Bucerius, M. (2006). Is speed of integration really a success factor of mergers and acquisitions? An analysis of the role of internal and external relatedness. *Strategic Management Journal , 27*, pp. 347-367.

Homburg, C., & Krohmer, H. (2006). *Marketingmanagement* (2 ed.). Wiesbaden: Gabler Verlag.

Imaa. (2013). *Imaa - institute of mergers, acquisitions and alliances.* Retrieved 05 25, 2013, from http://www.imaa-institute.org/statistics-mergers-acquisitions.html

Inkpen, A., Sundaram, A., & Rockwood, K. (2000). Cross-border acquisitions of U.S. technology assets. *California Management Review , 42* (3), pp. 50-71.

Isom, P., Madden, L., Moyers, M., & Tiemann, D. (2013). *2013 M&A outlook survey.* Delaware: KPGM LLP.

Jansen, S. A. (2001). *Merger & Acquisitions* (4 ed.). Wiesbaden: Springer Gabler Verlag.

Jansen, S. A. (2008). *Mergers & Acquisitions* (5 ed.). Wiesbaden: Springer Gabler Verlag.

Jensen, M. C., & Ruback, R. S. (1983). The market for corporate control: The scientific evidence. *Journal of Financial Economics , 11*, 5-50.

Kary, C. (2013, May 2). Mehr Rücktrittsklauseln, detailliertere Garantien. *Die Presse* , 11.

Kavanagh, M. H., & Askanasy, N. M. (2006). The impact of leadership and change management strategy on organizational culture and individual acceptance of change during a merger. *British Journal of Management , 17*, pp. 81-103.

Kenneth, D., & Harbir, S. (1994). Sources of acquisition cultural risk. In G. v. Krogh, A. Sinatra, & H. Singh, *The management of corporate acquisitions – international perspectives* (pp. 251-292). Houndsmills: Palgrave Macmillan.

King, Dalton, Daily, & Covin. (2004). Meta-analyses of post-acquisition performance: Indications of unidentified moderators. *Strategic Management Journal* , pp. 187-200.

Klarmann, M. (2008). *Methodische Problemfelder der Erfolgsfaktorenforschung – Bestandsaufnahme und empirische Analysen.* Wiesbaden: Gabler Verlag.

Kolesky, K. (2004). *Management kultureller Integrationsprozesse bei grenzüberschreitenden Unternehmenszusammenschlüssen – Eine Analyse westeuropäischer Akquisitionen in Osteuropa.* Kassel: Kassel Univ. Press.

Kunisch, S. (2008). M&A-Markt 2007 in Deutschland – Zwei unterschiedliche Jahreshälften. *M&A Review 2/2008* , pp. 57-65.

Larsson, R., & Finkelstein, S. (1999). Integrating strategic, organizational, and human resource perspectives on mergers and acquisitions: A case survey of synergy realization. *Organizational science , 10* (1), pp. 1-26.

Liao, N. N. (2004). On acculturation of business acquisition: The Case of two machine tool manufacturers in Taiwan. *The Journal of American Academy of Business , 4* (1), 233-243.

Marks, M. L., & Mirvis, P. H. (2010). *Joining forces: Marking one plus one equal three in meger and acquisitions.* San Francisco: Jossey-Bass.

Marks, M. L., & Mirvis, P. H. (2001). Making merger and acquisitions work: Strategic and psychological preperation. *Academy of Management Execuitve , 15* (2), 80-92.

Meffert, H., Burmann, C., & Kirchgeorg, M. (2008). *Marketing –Grundlagen marktorientierter Unternehmensführung – Konzepte – Instrumente-Praxisbeispiel* (10 ed.). Wiesbaden: Gabler Verlag.

Mergermarket. (2007). *M&A Integration In association with: A mergermarket report on issues surrounding post-deal integration for European companies.* London.

Mergermarket. (2013). *Statista*. Retrieved May 13, 2013, from http://www.statista.com/statistics/246721/percentage-of-global-munda-deals-by-type/

Meyer, C. B. (2008). Value leakages in mergers and acquisitions: Why they occur and how they can be addressed. *Long Range Planning , 41*, 197-224.

Morag, O., & Barakonyi, K. (2009). The influence of speed of integration on M&A integration success. *VEZETÈSTUDOMÀNY , 11*, pp. 55-59.

Nahass, G., Boyle, M., Smith, J., Balog, J., Kennedy, P., & Skorupka, D. (2008). *How can leadership make a difference? An integration survey 2008.* New York City: PricewaterhousCoopers.

Nahavandi, A., & Malekzadeh, A. R. (1988). Acculturation in merges and acquisitions. *Academy of Management Review , 13*, pp. 79-90.

Olie, R. (1994). Shades of culture and institutions in international mergers. *Organization Studies , 15* (3), pp. 381-405.

Pablo, A. L. (1994). Determinants of acquisition integration level: A decision-making perspective. *Academy of Management Journal , 37*, pp. 803-836.

Pack, H. (2000). Due diligence. In G. Picot, *Handbuch Mergers and Acquisitions* (pp. 221-254). Stuttgart: Schaeffer-Poeschl Verlag.

Picot, G. (2000). *Handbuch Merger & Acquisitons.* Stuttgart: Schaeffer-Poeschl Verlag .

Piske, R. (2002). German acquisitions in Poland: An empirical study on integration management and integration success. *Human Resource Development International , 5* (3), pp. 295-312.

Podsakoff, P. M., MacKenzie, S. B., Lee, J.-Y., & Podsakoff, N. P. (2003). Common method bias in behavioural research: A critical review of the literature and recommended remedies. *Journal of Applied Psychology , 88*, pp. 869-903.

Puranam, P., & Srikanth, K. (2007). What they know vs. what they do: How acquirers leverage technology acquisitions. *Strategic Management Journal , 28*, 805-825.

Puranam, P., Singh, H., & Chaudhuri, S. (2009). Integrating acquired capabilities: When structural integration is (un)necessary. *Organization Sience , 20* (2), pp. 313-328.

Puranam, P., Singh, H., & Zollo, M. (2006). Organizing for innovation: Managing the coordination-autonomy dilemma in technology acquisitions. *Academy of Management Journal , 49* (2), 263-280.

Ranft, A. L., & Lord, M. D. (2002). Acquiring new technologies and capabilities: A grounded model of acquisition implementation. *Organization Science , 13* (4), pp. 420-441.
Rhodes-Kropf, M., & Viswanathan, S. (2004). Market valuation and merger. *The Journal of Finance , LIX*, pp. 2685-2718.

Schlaepfer, R., di Paola, S., Kupiers, R., Brauchli-Rohrer, B., Marti, A., Brun, P., et al. (2008). *How can leadership make a difference - An integration Survey.* PWC.

Schlüzen, U., & Jöns, I. (2003, Vol. 1). Die Bedeutung und Gestaltung der Integrationsgeschwindigkeit bei Fusionen und Akquisitionen. *Mannheimer Beiträge zur Wirtschafts- und Organisationspsychologie* , pp. 3-9.

Schweiger, D. M., & Goulet, P. K. (2005). Facilitating acquisition integration through deep-level cultural learning interventions: A longitudinal field experiment. *Organization Studies , 26* (10), pp. 1477-1499.

Schweiger, D. M., & Very, P. (2003). Creating value through merger and acquisition integration. In S. Finkelstein, & C. Cooper, *Advances in merger and acquisitions* (pp. 1-26). Bingley, UK: Emerald Group Publishing Limited.

Schweiger, D. M., & Weber, Y. (1989). Strategies for managing human resources during mergers and acquisitions: An empirical investigation. *Human Resource Planning Journal , 12* (2), pp. 69-86.

Seo, M.-G., & Hill, S. N. (2005). Understanding the Human Side of Merger and Acquisition. *The Journal of Applied Behavioral Science , 41* (4), 422-443.

Sharan, V. (2003). *International business: Concept, environment and strategy* (2 ed.). Singapore: Pearson.

Sherer, J. (1994). Corporate Cultures: Turning us versus them into we. *Hospitals and Health Networks , 9*, pp. 20-27.

Shrivastava, P. (1986). Postmerger integration. *The Journal of Business Strategy , 7* (1), pp. 65-76.

Singh, H., & Montgomery, C. A. (1987). Corporate acquisition strategies and economic perfomance . *Strategic Management Journal , 8* (4), 377- 386.

Slangen, A. H. (2006). National cultural distance and initial foreign acquisition performance: The moderating effect of integration. *The Journal of World Business , 41* (2), 161-170.

Stahl, G. K., & Voigt, A. (2008). Do cultural differences matter in mergers and acquisitions? *Organization Science , 19* (1), pp. 160–176.

Sudman, S., & Bradburn, N. (1973). Effect on time and memory factors on response in surveys. *Journal of the American Statistical Association , 68* (344), 805-815.

Tajfel, H. (1981). *Human groups and social categories.* Cambridge, UK: Cambridge University Press.

Teerikangas, S., & Very, P. (2006). The culture-performance relationship in M&A: From yes/no to how. *British Journal of Management , 17*, pp. 31-48.

Turner, J. (1982). Toward a cognitive redefinition of the social group. In H. Tajfel, *Social Identity and Intergroup Relations* (pp. 15–40.). Cambridge, UK: Cambridge University Press.

Vermeulen, F., & Barkema, H. (2001). Learning through acquisition. *Academic Management Journal , 44*, pp. 457-476.

Voss, I., & Müller-Stewens, G. (2006). Strategische M&A-Kompetenz imRahmen von Akquisitionsstrategien – Komponenten, Erfolgsfaktoren und Aufbau. In F. Keuper, M. Häfner, & C. v. Glahn, *Der M&A-Prozess – Konzepte, Ansätze und Strategien für die Pre- und Post-* (pp. 3-32). Wiesbaden: Gabler Verlag.

Walter, G. A., & Barney, J. B. (1990). Management objectives in merger and acquisitions. *Strategic Management Journal , 11*, pp. 79-86.

Weber, R. A., & Camerer, C. F. (2003). Cultural conflict and merger failure: An experimental approach. *Management Science , 49* (4), 400–415.

Weber, Y., Shenkar, O., & Raveh, A. (1996). National and corporate cultural fit in mergers/acquisitions: An exploratory study. *Management Science , 42* (8), pp. 1215-1227.

Weston, F. J., Mitchell, M. L., & Mulherin, H. J. (2004). *Takeovers,restructuring, and corporate governance – international edition* (4 ed.). New Jersey: Pearson .

Wille, C., Bauer, F., & Anslinger, T. (2011). Corporate Brand Management bei Mergers & Acquisitions. In J. Wollersheim, & E. Barthel, *Forum Mergers & Acquisitions 2011* (pp. 139-178). Wiesbaden.

Wirtz, B. W. (2012). *Merger & Acquisitions Management: Stratgie und Organisation von Unternehmenszusammenschluessen* (2 ed.). Wiesbaden: Gabler Verlag Springer Fachmedien.

Zollo, M., & Meier, D. (2008). What is M&A perfomance? *Academy of Management Journal , 22*, pp. 55-77.

Zollo, M., & Singh, H. (2004). Deliberate learning in corporate acquisitions:Post-acquisition strategies and integration capability in U.S. bank mergers. *Strategic Management Journal* , *25*, 1233-1256.

Appendix

Appendix A: Common Method Bias Analysis

Total Variance						
Items	Eigenvalue			Sum of squared loadings for extraction		
	Total	% of variance	cumulative %	Total	% of variance	cumulative %
1	7.139	28.555	28.555	7.139	28.555	28.555
2	4.811	19.244	47.799	4.811	19.244	47.799
3	2.404	9.616	57.415	2.404	9.616	57.415
4	1.407	5.627	63.042	1.407	5.627	63.042
5	1.282	5.128	68.169	1.282	5.128	68.169
6	.986	3.944	72.114			
7	.885	3.540	75.654			
8	.770	3.079	78.733			
9	.706	2.824	81.556			
10	.559	2.235	83.792			
11	.502	2.006	85.798			
12	.473	1.893	87.691			
13	.433	1.732	89.423			
14	.375	1.502	90.925			
15	.364	1.457	92.381			
16	.327	1.306	93.688			
17	.294	1.176	94.864			
18	.268	1.073	95.937			
19	.223	.890	96.827			
20	.201	.805	97.633			
21	.182	.727	98.360			
22	.137	.547	98.906			
23	.126	.502	99.409			
24	.081	.324	99.733			
25	.067	.267	100.000			

Appendix B: Cover Letter

Innsbruck, 18.02.2013

Forschungsprojekt „Werthebel bei Mergers & Acquisitions"

Sehr geehrter HerrSchweickardt,

die **Universität Innsbruck** und das **MCI Management Center**haben im November 2012 das SMA-Research Lab mit dem Ziel, ein besseres und ganzheitlicheres Verständnis für die Phänomene **Strategie, Mergers & Acquisitions** zu generieren, gegründet. Zweck des **SMA-Research Lab** ist es, einen hochwertigen Beitrag für die Wissenschaft durch **Kooperationen**, Publikationen und Konferenzbeiträge zu leisten. Zudem soll ein starker **Praxistransfer** durch Projekte mit Unternehmen und praxisnahen Verbänden erreicht werden.

Da sich die **Erfolgsquoten** von Unternehmenstransaktionen in den vergangenen Jahren kaum gebessert haben, sollen im Rahmen dieser Untersuchung zentrale **Werthebel** von M&A-Transaktionen untersucht werden. Zu diesem Zweck kontaktieren wir ca. 800 Käuferunternehmen im deutschsprachigen Raum, welche nach unseren Informationen (Zephyr-Datenbank) im Zeitraum vom 01.01.2007 bis 31.12.2010 an M&A-Transaktionen beteiligt waren.

Da Ihr Unternehmen in oben genanntem Zeitraum in einen Transaktionsprozess involviert war, möchten wir Sie bitten, uns durch Ihre **Teilnahme** an der Befragung, welche maximal 10-15 Minuten Ihrer Zeit in Anspruch nimmt, zu **unterstützen.** Sie können den Fragebogen per Post (im beiliegenden Rückantwortkouvert), per Fax oder per Mail zurücksenden bzw. online ausfüllen (www.sma-research.org).

Als **Dankeschön** für Ihre Unterstützung erhalten Sie - falls gewünscht - die Untersuchungsergebnisse. Darüber hinaus stehen wir Ihnen für eine **Diskussion der Ergebnisse** gerne zur Verfügung.

Alle Daten werden selbstverständlich **strengvertraulich** und ausschließlich zu **wissenschaftlichen Zwecken** verwendet. Alle weiteren Informationen zum Ausfüllen finden Sie im Fragebogen selbst.

universität innsbruck

Herzlichen Dank bereits im Voraus für Ihre Teilnahme und Unterstützung!
Mit freundlichen Grüßen aus Innsbruck

Dr. Florian Bauer
Lektor und Direktor SMA Research Lab
Department Management & Recht
Tel: -3622, Fax: -3699
florian.bauer@sma-resarch.org

Univ.-Prof. Dr. Kurt Matzler
Institut für strategisches Management,
Marketing &Tourismus
Universität Innsbruck
www.sma-research.org

Appendix C: Questionnaire

MCI® MANAGEMENT CENTER INNSBRUCK

] sma research lab [
research & practice for strategy, mergers and acqusitions

M&A-Management*

Phasenübergreifende Wertsteigerungsmechanismen und Interdependenzen bei M&A

Forschungsprojekt

Gegenstand der Studie vom SMA Research Lab und fünf Masterstudierenden ist die phasenübergreifende Analyse von Wertsteigerungsmechanismen und Interdependenzen bei M&A.

Ihr Nutzen

Selbstverständlich können Sie auf Ihren Wunsch hin die Ergebnisse dieser Untersuchung erhalten. Gerne stehen wir Ihnen auch für weitere Fragen persönlich zur Verfügung.

Ihre Ansprechpartner – das Forscherteam

Benedikt Bergmeister:
Master-Student am Institut für Strategisches Management an der Leopold-Franzens Universität Innsbruck
Thema der Masterarbeit:
The Impact of Continuity and Communication on Cultural and Task Integration in M&As.

Mai Anh Dao:
Master-Studentin am Institut für Strategisches Management an der Leopold-Franzens Universität Innsbruck
Thema der Masterarbeit:
The Common Ground Phenomenon and Its Influence on Cultural and Task Integration

Caroline Proft:
Master-Studentin im Studiengang „International Business and Law" am Management Center Innsbruck
Thema der Masterarbeit:
The Effects of Speed of Integration on the M&A.Outcome

Nicole Rudolf:
Master-Studentin am Institut für Strategisches Management an der Universität Innsbruck
Thema der Masterarbeit:
The Value Creating Mechanisms of Ambidexterity in M&A

Melanie Waschak:
Master-Studentin im Studiengang „International Business and Law" am Management Center Innsbruck
Thema der Masterarbeit:
Decision Making Style and its Influence on Cultural and Task Integration Speed

KONTAKTDATEN:
SMA Research Lab
Universitätsstraße 15
A-6020 Innsbruck
Tel.: +43 512 2070 3634
Mail: request@sma-research.org

Was ist beim Ausfüllen zu beachten

Alle Informationen werden selbstverständlich **vollständig anonymisiert** und **streng vertraulich behandelt**. Ein Rückschluss auf Sie bzw. ein bestimmtes Unternehmen ist nicht möglich.

Bitte beantworten Sie den Fragebogen nur, wenn Sie bereits vor **Abschluss der Transaktion** beim Käuferunternehmen gearbeitet haben. Falls dies nicht der Fall sein sollte, möchten wir Sie bitten, den Fragebogen an eine **entsprechende Person** in Ihrem Unternehmen weiterzuleiten. Besten Dank!

Bitte lassen Sie keine Frage bei der Beantwortung aus. Ein guter Schätzwert ist ebenfalls sehr wertvoll für die Untersuchung. Falls Sie an mehreren M&A-Transaktionen beteiligt waren, beziehen Sie sich bitte auf einen konkreten Fall.

Die Beantwortung der Fragen erfordert zwischen **10 und maximal 15 Minuten** Ihrer Zeit. Gerne kann die Beantwortung auch telefonisch im Rahmen eines Gespräches erfolgen. Hierfür würden wir Sie um Kontaktaufnahme unter der oben angegebenen Adresse bitten.

Herzlichen Dank für Ihre Unterstützung!

*Diese empirische Untersuchung ist Teil eines vom Tiroler Wissenschaftsfonds geförderten Forschungsprojekts.

ABSCHNITT I: Fragen zur Pre-Merger-Phase

In diesem Abschnitt werden die Ähnlichkeit in Bezug auf strategische Ausrichtung, Aufgaben- und Teamorientierung sowie die Interaktionen der beteiligten Unternehmen abgefragt.

In Bezug auf den strategischen und kulturellen Fit, wie gut passten Käufer- und Zielunternehmen hinsichtlich folgender Kriterien zusammen?

Wie gut passten die an der Transaktion beteiligten Unternehmen in Bezug auf folgende Punkte zusammen?	1 (Unternehmen passten überhaupt nicht zusammen)	2	3	4	5 (Unternehmen passten sehr gut zusammen)
Einführung neuer Produktgenerationen	■	■	■	■	■
Erweiterung der Produktpalette	■	■	■	■	■
Erschließung neuer Märkte	■	■	■	■	■
Eintritt in neue Technologiefelder	■	■	■	■	■
Optimierung bestehender Produktqualität	■	■	■	■	■
Optimierung der Produktionsflexibilität	■	■	■	■	■
Senkung der Produktionskosten	■	■	■	■	■
Optimierung des Materialverbrauchs und/oder Gewinnoptimierung	■	■	■	■	■

Wie gut passten die an der Transaktion beteiligten Unternehmen in Bezug auf die folgenden Eigenschaften zusammen?		1 (Unternehmen passten überhaupt nicht zusammen)	2	3	4	5 (Unternehmen passten sehr gut zusammen)
Aufgaben-orientierung	Das Verständnis der Mitarbeiter für ihre eigenen Arbeitsprozesse	■	■	■	■	■
	Das Verständnis der Mitarbeiter für Prozesse im Gesamtunternehmen	■	■	■	■	■
	Das Verständnis der Mitarbeiter für die Unternehmensstrategie	■	■	■	■	■
	Das Verständnis der Mitarbeiter für die Aufgaben anderer Abteilungen	■	■	■	■	■
	Das Verständnis der Mitarbeiter für die Wettbewerbssituation des Unternehmens	■	■	■	■	■
Team-orientierung	Die Art der Mitarbeiter miteinander zu kommunizieren	■	■	■	■	■
	Die Rolle der Führungskräfte gegenüber ihren Mitarbeitern	■	■	■	■	■
	Der Umgang der Mitarbeiter miteinander in ihrer Freizeit (z.B. Sport)	■	■	■	■	■
	Die gegenseitige Hilfe von Mitarbeitern bei der Arbeit	■	■	■	■	■
	Das Verständnis der Mitarbeiter über Qualifikationen der Kollegen	■	■	■	■	■
	Das Verständnis der Mitarbeiter über persönliche Hintergründe der Kollegen (z.B. Familie, Hobbies, Gewohnheiten)	■	■	■	■	■

Interaktion der Unternehmen vor der Transaktion

Inwieweit haben Käufer- und Zielunternehmen in Bezug auf die folgenden Kriterien bereits vor der Transaktion zusammengearbeitet?	1 (Gar nicht)	2	3	4	5 (Sehr intensiv)
Gemeinsame Projekte (z.B. Forschungsprojekte)	■	■	■	■	■
Mitarbeiteraustausch (z.B. für Schulungen)	■	■	■	■	■
Gemeinsame Marktbearbeitung (z.B. Distributionskanäle)	■	■	■	■	■
Marketing (z. B. gemeinsame Werbung)	■	■	■	■	■
Einkauf (z.B. Einkaufsgemeinschaft)	■	■	■	■	■
Gemeinsame/gegenseitige Investitionen	■	■	■	■	■

2

ABSCHNITT II: Fragen zur Post-Merger-Phase (1)

In diesem Abschnitt geht es um die Harmonisierung der an der Transaktion beteiligten Unternehmen, die Integrationsgeschwindigkeit sowie um Koordinationsmechanismen.

In welchem Umfang wurden folgende Punkte beim Zielunternehmen verändert?

Wie beurteilen Sie die Veränderung in folgenden Bereichen:		1 Keinerlei Veränderung	2	3	4 Teilweise Veränderung	5	6	7 Vollkommene Veränderung
Soziokulturelle-Integrationsebene	Organisationsstruktur	■	■	■	■	■	■	■
	Organisationskultur (z.B. Vision, Leitbild)	■	■	■	■	■	■	■
	Personalmanagement (HR)	■	■	■	■	■	■	■
Integration der Produktion	Produktion	■	■	■	■	■	■	■
	Beschaffung	■	■	■	■	■	■	■
Marketing-Integration	Distributionskanäle	■	■	■	■	■	■	■
	Sales/After-Sales Service	■	■	■	■	■	■	■
	Marketingprogramm	■	■	■	■	■	■	■
System-Integration	Strategische Planungssysteme	■	■	■	■	■	■	■
	Finanzsysteme	■	■	■	■	■	■	■
	Management-Informationssysteme	■	■	■	■	■	■	■

Welchen Einfluss hatte die Akquisition auf die Mitarbeiter beider Unternehmen in der Integrationsphase?

Für viele Mitarbeiter...	1 Stimme gar nicht zu	2	3	4 neutral	5	6	7 Stimme vollkommen zu
...hatte die Akquisition radikale Veränderungen des **Arbeitsalltags** zur Folge.	■	■	■	■	■	■	■
...hatte die Akquisition radikale Veränderungen im **privaten Bereich** zur Folge.	■	■	■	■	■	■	■
...führte die Akquisition **ganz allgemein** zu radikalen Veränderungen.	■	■	■	■	■	■	■

Wie schnell wurden die einzelnen Ebenen harmonisiert?

Bitte geben Sie Dauer der Integration von 1 = „Länger als 24 Monate"; 2 = „22-24 Monate"; 3 = „18-21 Monate"; 4 = „14-17 Monate"; 5 = „10-13 Monate"; 6 = „6-9 Monate"; 7 = „weniger als 6 Monate" an.

Integrationsdauer	1 Länger als 24 Monate	2	3	4	5	6	7 Weniger als 6 Monate
Dauer der soziokulturellen Integration (Org.-struktur, Org.-kultur, HR)	■	■	■	■	■	■	■
Dauer der Integration der Produktion	■	■	■	■	■	■	■
Dauer der Marketingintegration	■	■	■	■	■	■	■
Dauer der System-Integration (Strategische-, Finanz- und Mgmt.-Info.-Systeme)	■	■	■	■	■	■	■

Begleitende Unterstützung und Kommunikationsintensität während der Integration

Wie beurteilen Sie das Ausmaß der folgenden Maßnahmen?	1 Keinerlei	2	3	4 Ausreichend	5	6	7 Sehr umfangreich
Ausmaß an begleitender Unterstützung durch das Management (z.B. Training, Job rotation, etc.)	■	■	■	■	■	■	■
Ausmaß an Kommunikation notwendiger Informationen	■	■	■	■	■	■	■

ABSCHNITT II: Fragen zur Post-Merger-Phase (2)

Welche Rolle spielte Kommunikation in der Integrationsphase?

Bei der beschriebenen Transaktion war es besonders wichtig, unsere(n) Mitarbeiter(n)...	1 Stimme überhaupt nicht zu	2	3	4 Neutral	5	6	7 Stimme vollkommen zu
...mit **detaillierten** Informationen zu versorgen	■	■	■	■	■	■	■
...**gut verständliche** Informationen zu kommunizieren	■	■	■	■	■	■	■
...**ehrlich** über die Bedeutung der Akquisition für deren Zukunft zu informieren	■	■	■	■	■	■	■
...den **Grund** für die Akquisition zu erläutern	■	■	■	■	■	■	■
...Informationen über den **Nutzen** der Akquisition zu liefern	■	■	■	■	■	■	■
...zu informieren, wie sie ihre **Meinungen und Vorschläge** äußern können	■	■	■	■	■	■	■
...Informationen über die **Vision und die Unternehmenskultur** zu vermitteln	■	■	■	■	■	■	■
...**aktiv** die neuen Arbeitsweisen und -methoden zu erörtern	■	■	■	■	■	■	■

Entscheidungsverhalten in der Integrationsphase

Entscheidungen, welche die Integration betrafen...	1 Stimme überhaupt nicht zu	2	3	4 Neutral	5	6	7 Stimme vollkommen zu
...wurden gründlich durchdacht	■	■	■	■	■	■	■
...basierten auf Gefühlen, Wissen über Menschen und Lebenserfahrung	■	■	■	■	■	■	■
...wurden genau geplant, nichts wurde dem Zufall überlassen	■	■	■	■	■	■	■
...wurden mit Bauchgefühl gefällt und waren meist genauso passend wie nach intensiven Analyse	■	■	■	■	■	■	■
...wurden erst nachdem die Integrationsziele detailliert definiert waren, getroffen.	■	■	■	■	■	■	■
...waren meist durch Emotionen gesteuert	■	■	■	■	■	■	■
...wurden mit Bedacht auf alle Details und Fakten getroffen	■	■	■	■	■	■	■
...wurden auf Basis von Erfahrung, Allgemeinwissen und Intuition getroffen	■	■	■	■	■	■	■

ABSCHNITT III: Erfolgsbeurteilung der integrierten Gesamtheit (1)

In welchem Ausmaß stimmen Sie den folgenden Aussagen zu?

	1 Stimme überhaupt nicht zu	2	3	4 Neutral	5	6	7 Stimme vollkommen zu
Die gesteckten Ziele wurden erreicht	■	■	■	■	■	■	■
Die Akquisition war die richtige unternehmerische Entscheidung	■	■	■	■	■	■	■
Bei einer Gesamtbetrachtung war die Akquisition ein Erfolg	■	■	■	■	■	■	■
Dem Unternehmen geht es nach der Akquisition besser als vorher	■	■	■	■	■	■	■

Nach der Transaktion...	1 Stimme überhaupt nicht zu	2	3	4 Neutral	5	6	7 Stimme vollkommen zu
...waren wir besser in der Einführung neuer Produkte	■	■	■	■	■	■	■
...waren wir besser in der Erweiterung unserer Produktpalette	■	■	■	■	■	■	■
...waren wir besser in der Erschließung neuer Märkte	■	■	■	■	■	■	■
...konnten wir neue Technologien besser nutzen	■	■	■	■	■	■	■
...konnte die Produktqualität verbessert werden	■	■	■	■	■	■	■
...konnte die Produktionsflexibilität gesteigert werden	■	■	■	■	■	■	■
...konnten die Produktionskosten minimiert werden	■	■	■	■	■	■	■
...konnte der Gewinn optimiert werden	■	■	■	■	■	■	■

4

ABSCHNITT III: Erfolgsbeurteilung der integrierten Gesamtheit (2)

Inwieweit haben sich die folgenden Größen nach der Transaktion verändert?

Bitte schätzen Sie die Veränderung nach der Transaktion von 1 = „Stark verschlechtert" über 4 = „Keine Veränderung" bis 7 = „Stark verbessert" in Bezug auf die folgenden Größen ab.

Wie haben sich die folgenden Größen entwickelt?	1 Stark verschlechtert	2	3	4 Keine Veränderungen	5	6	7 Stark verbessert
Gesamtkapitalrentabilität (Return on Investment, ROI)	■	■	■	■	■	■	■
Eigenkapitalrentabilität (Return on Equity, ROE)	■	■	■	■	■	■	■
Umsatzrendite (Return on Sales, ROS)	■	■	■	■	■	■	■
Relativer Unternehmenswert	■	■	■	■	■	■	■
Umsatz (verglichen zur Ausgangssituation vor der Akquisition)	■	■	■	■	■	■	■
Marktanteil (verglichen zur Ausgangssituation vor der Akquisition)	■	■	■	■	■	■	■

Vergleich von prognostizierten und tatsächlichen Markt- und Absatzgrößen

Bitte schätzen Sie ein, inwieweit die tatsächlich erreichten Verkaufszahlen und Gesamtmarkterfolge von den am Tag der Zusammenführung prognostizierten Voraussagen abweichen, von 1 = „stark negativ" über 4 = „keine Abweichung" bis 7 = „stark positiv".

	1 Stark negative Abweichung	2	3	4 Keine Abweichung	5	6	7 Stark positive Abweichung
Tatsächlicher Marktanteil im Vergleich zur Prognose	■	■	■	■	■	■	■
Tatsächliche Verkaufszahlen im Vergleich zur Prognose	■	■	■	■	■	■	■

Veränderungen bei Wissenstransfer, sowie Produkt- bzw. Prozessinnovationen

Bitte geben Sie an, ob sich Wissenstransfer und unerwarteter Anstieg an Produkt- bzw. Prozessinnovationen ereignet hat, von 1 = „keinerlei Anstieg" über 4 = „teilweise Anstieg" bis 7 = „starker Anstieg" in Bezug auf folgende Größen ab.

	1 Keinerlei Anstieg	2	3	4 Teilweise Anstieg	5	6	7 Starker Anstieg
Austausch an Technologie- und Know-how für bestimmte Produktkategorien	■	■	■	■	■	■	■
Steigerung an nicht eingeplanten Produkt- und Prozessinnovationen	■	■	■	■	■	■	■

ABSCHNITT IV: Sonstige Angaben (1)

Bitte beurteilen Sie zum Abschluss die folgenden Größen

Bitte beurteilen Sie die relative Größe des Zielunternehmens im Vergleich zum Käuferunternehmen in Bezug auf den Umsatz im Jahr vor der Transaktion

■ < 25% ■ 25%-49% ■ 50%-74%
■ 75%-100% ■ > 100%

Bitte beurteilen Sie das durchschnittliche Branchenwachstum der letzten drei Jahre vor der Transaktion

■ > - 15% ■ - 15% bis – 5% ■ - 5% bis +/- 0% ■ +/- 0% bis 5%
■ 5% bis 10% ■ 11%-20% ■ 21% bis 30% ■ > 30 %

Bitte geben Sie die aktuelle Höhe des Jahresumsatzes des fusionierten Unternehmens nach der Transaktion an

■ < 25 Mio. € ■ 25-49 Mio. € ■ 50-99 Mio. € ■ 100-249 Mio. €
■ 250-499 Mio. € ■ 500-1.000 Mio. € ■ > 1.000 Mio. €

In welcher Branche ist Ihr Unternehmen tätig? ■ --

Sitz des Zielunternehmens:

■ Deutschland ■ Österreich
■ Schweiz ■ Andere: ------------------------

Sitz des Käuferunternehmens: --

Art der Transaktion: ■ **Horizontal** ■ **Vertikal** ■ **Konglomerat**

In welchem Jahr wurde die beschriebene Transaktion durchgeführt? ------------------------------

ABSCHNITT IV: Sonstige Angaben (2)

Bitte geben Sie zum Abschluss Auskunft zu folgenden Punkten

Welche Position innerhalb des Unternehmens haben Sie aktuell? ------------------------------------

Wie viele Jahre Erfahrung haben Sie in dieser Branche? --

Wie lange arbeiten Sie bereits für diesen Betrieb? ■ < 1 Jahr ■ 2-4 Jahre ■ 4-6 Jahre ■ 6-8 Jahre ■ 8-10 Jahre ■ < 10 Jahre

Um welche Transaktionsart handelte es sich? ■ Fusion ■ Unternehmenskauf

Wie viele Transaktionen hat ihr Unternehmen in den fünf Jahren vor der beschriebenen Transaktion durchgeführt? ■ keine ■ 1-2 ■ 3-4 ■ 5-6 ■ > 7

Zielmärkte Käuferunternehmen: ■ B2B ■ B2C ■ beide | Zielmärkte Zielunternehmen: ■ B2B ■ B2C ■ beide

Diese Seite wird selbstverständlich vor der Auswertung der inhaltlichen Fragen vom Fragebogen getrennt

Interesse an den Untersuchungsergebnissen: ■

Bereitschaft, an weiteren Untersuchungen des Departments teilzunehmen: ■

Sollten Sie oben Ihr Interesse bekundet haben, so bitten wir Sie, die folgenden Angaben zu machen:

Anrede: ■ Frau ■ Herr

Titel: ■ Prof. ■ Dr. ■ Mag. ■ Master ■ Bachelor

Vor- und Nachname: --

E-Mail-Adresse: --

Fax-Nummer (optional): --

Herzlichen Dank für Ihre Unterstützung!

Diese Seite wird selbstverständlich vor der Auswertung der inhaltlichen Fragen vom Fragebogen getrennt

MIX
Papier aus verantwortungsvollen Quellen
Paper from responsible sources
FSC® C105338

If you have any concerns about our products,
you can contact us on
ProductSafety@springernature.com

In case Publisher is established outside the EU,
the EU authorized representative is:
Springer Nature Customer Service Center GmbH
Europaplatz 3, 69115 Heidelberg, Germany

Printed by Libri Plureos GmbH
in Hamburg, Germany